Celtic Christianity

Celtic Christianity

Ecology and
Holiness

An anthology by
William Parker Marsh
and Christopher Bamford

Inner Traditions  Lindisfarne Press

Celtic Christianity originally appeared as *Lindisfarne Letter 13*
© 1982 The Lindisfarne Association
The Heritage of Celtic Christianity: Ecology and Holiness
© 1982 Christopher Bamford
The Holy Isles © 1982 Kathleen Raine
This edition © 1987 The Lindisfarne Press

An Inner Traditions/Lindisfarne Press Book

Published by the Lindisfarne Press, PO Box 127, West
Stockbridge, MA 01266.
Distributed to the book trade by Inner Traditions International.
All inquiries regarding distribution should be addressed to Inner
Traditions International, Park Street, Rochester, VT 05767.

ISBN 0–89281–079–3

Printed in Great Britain

Contents

Ecology and holiness
The heritage of Celtic Christianity

Christopher Bamford

High Cross of Monasterboice

The Maker of all things,
The Lord God worship we:
Heaven white with angels' wings,
Earth and the white-waved sea.
Early Irish Poem

This much the lettered men, scribes and exegetes find writ
in sacral membrana, the historia of our kings, sayings
of our prophets, and ta kronika and we that be unlettered,
hear what is handed down in tellings told by baldheads
to their beardless kin.

But be that as it may, if that vast oak had not the
bright-berried growth intwined upon it, which
flowering, so I've heard tell, the filid, vates or druidae
(a kind of Levitic priesthood among the Galatic people)
do cut with a golden sickle at certain times in their year
of Luna months.

That great lignum arbor una nobilis within the inmost
nemeton of this wild Ephraim holt, had for Golden
Bough the pierced & hanging son of the Lord of Salem.

David Jones, The Kensington Mass

Christians of all persuasions have always loved the
saints of the Celtic Church and the traditions of sanc-
tity, learning and stewardship for which they stood;
and the Celtic or, as it is also called, the British Church
has always represented an ideal for those who have

known of it, and not simply as a Golden Age of innocence and purity which, in the words of Nora Chadwick, has "never been surpassed and perhaps been equalled only by the ascetics of the eastern deserts,"[1] but also, and more importantly, as an alternative seed, "a light from the west," perhaps obscure and even alien, but nevertheless powerful and true with the kind of reality we seem to need today. "If the British Church had survived," wrote H. J. Massingham, "it is possible that the fissure between Christianity and nature, widening through the centuries, would not have cracked the unity of western man's attitude to the universe."[2]

This combination of saintliness and ecology is but one aspect of the heritage. The other is made up of the sacred and secular traditions of learning, science, poetry and art, which were seen as the essential concomitants, the frame and the vehicle, whereby God's purpose for the cosmos, its transfiguration, might be aided and fulfilled.

The difficulty, of course, is that the heritage sought for is that of a beginning — which, as beginning, is shrouded in mystery, is quintessentially mysterious: beginning in mystery, continuing in mystery, ending in mystery. One gets the sense, indeed, trying to unravel the different strands of scholarship, legend and archaeology, of entering into relation with a moment of history in which the spiritual is so closely and clearly involved with the phenomenal that all of one's usual means of understanding are wanting. "The loom may be of this world," J. W. Taylor wrote, "but the tapestry, the colours and the inscription on it are only partly of this world. They belong essentially to the spiritual and the heavenly."[3] The point is, I think, that all beginnings, all seeds, are thus mysterious, and so constitute insoluble *aporia* for the merely empirical scholar.

In this instance, it is the coming of Christianity to, and the Christianity of, Ireland and England that is the great question. In the sixth century, the great Welsh bard Taliesin claimed: "Christ, the Word from the beginning, was from the beginning our Teacher, and we never lost his teaching. Christianity was in Asia a new thing; but there never was a time when the Druids of Britain held not its doctrines."[4] There, perfectly posed, is the first quandary. We do not know when or how Christianity first arrived at those westernmost reaches. It seems always to have been there. Legend tells us, for instance, that Irish sages attended the events on Golgotha "in the spirit" and felt, by what means we cannot tell, "the groans and travails of creation cease." Yeats notes a similar story in which on the day of the Crucifixion King Conchubar and Bucrach the Leinster Druid are sitting together. Conchubar notices "the unusual changes of the creation and the eclipse of the sun and the moon at its full"; he asks the Druid the cause of these signs, and Bucrach replies, "Jesus Christ, the Son of God, who is now being crucified by the Jews."[5]

Another legend is that associated with Saint Bridgit or Bride. It tells how Bride, a child so young she could neither walk nor talk, was cast adrift in a coracle and came to land at Iona, where she began to walk and talk, singing:

I am but a little child,
Yet my mantle shall be laid
On the Lord of the World.
The King of the Elements Himself
Shall rest upon my heart,
And I will give Him Peace.[6]

The legend goes on to tell how she was brought up by Druids, until one day she was led by a white dove, through a grove of rowans, to a parched, desert land. There, in a stable, she assisted as "aid-woman" or midwife at the birth of a Holy Child upon whose brow she placed three drops of holy water to unite him with the earth. Then, because the cows in that desert land had no milk on account of the drought, Bride sang "runes of paradise" to them so that milk flowed freely, and the Holy Child could drink of earthly produce — wrapped in Bride's blue mantle, close to her heart. Thus, Bride was called: aid-woman of Mary, foster-mother of Christ, godmother of the Son of God.

Now Bride is, in this, a part mythological figure, assimilable to Artemis, aid-woman to Leto in the birth of Apollo, and to the northern Goddess Brigantia, and the Celtic Bridghe, Goddess of knowledge and life, mother of poets. But, before jumping to rather obvious conclusions, two further aspects of the legend must be borne in mind. First, there is a future Bride, or rather, perhaps, Bride is "once and future" and her task is not yet complete. Namely, it is said that another Bride will come to bind His hair and wash His feet, and perhaps even to be the Bride of Christ Himself. This Bride is Sophia, surely, the Virgin Wisdom of the World. But there is yet another Bride, this time solidly historical, who ranks with Saints Patrick and Columba in Ireland's great Triad of Saints.[7]

I quote these stories to suggest that Celtic tradition experienced a continuity in cosmic process, that extended from its inception, Creation, to its conclusion, Deification. For the Celt, therefore, Christianity and the act of Christ was never an end in itself, but rather was always experienced as a divine means to the true end. God's purpose from which he never deviated though humanity and creation fell, namely, that he should be "all in all." Christ's death and resurrection was thus seen as a healing mediation, a balm, that made possible once again the original dream of paradise, the reconciliation of humanity and nature in God. It is in this sense that Christianity, as the true end for which creation was intended, was always in Ireland and that to seek its historical beginning there is vain. Another legend bears this out. It is said that when Lucifer tempted our forebears in paradise, the earth was already in existence, awaiting, as it were, the exile. But in this earth, the legend goes on, Ireland was already different: it was not just another part of earth, but rather that part of earth that paradise, before the Fall, had made its own. Paradise, that is, created for itself an image on earth before Lucifer ever entered into it; and that image was Ireland. No wonder then that paradise, or First Nature, was said to be more easily discerned there.

The question of Christianity in England is equally unsettled. Gildas wrote in the sixth century: "These islands received the beams of light . . . in the latter part of the reign of Tiberius Caesar, in whose time this religion was propagated without impediment or death."[8] The point about this is that Tiberius died in AD 37. Nor does Eusebius contradict this date, though scholars of course have difficulty explaining it. Nevertheless, by AD 199 Tertullian, listing the many peoples to whom the religion of Christ has come, can include, "the places of the Britons, which are inaccessible to the Romans." That is, if Christianity was in England by then it was not necessarily the Romans who brought it. The Gauls already had a bishop, Irenaeus of Lyons, of the line of St John, and one may assume much interchange between Gaul and Britain. There is, further, some evidence of a King Lucius at this time "bestowing

13

the freedom of country and nation with privilege of judgment and surety on all those who might be of the faith of Christ." It is also claimed for Lucius that he built the first church — around the year 200. And certainly one hundred years later, during the Diocletian persecutions, there were English martyrs — St Alban for instance; while in 314, at the Council of Arles, there were three British signatories, bishops, which already indicates a sizeable flock and tells us nothing of origins.[9]

The fundamental story here returns us to the pre AD 37 date given by Gildas, or close to it: in other words to the murky waters of St Joseph of Arimathea and Glastonbury. Joseph's name occurs in traditions in different places. We can track him through Provence, Aquitaine, Brittany and into Cornwall. At none of these, however, is he recorded as having stopped: he passes through them. His only stopping place, the term of his journey, according to legend, is Glastonbury. Here, on the Isle of Avalon, St Joseph with twelve companions and bearing the Holy Grail, the sacred vessel containing the blood and the sweat of Christ, settled and built a round church of mud and wattles. Now, the route he seems to have taken, up from Marseilles, along the Rhône to Limoges, and on to Brittany and Cornwall, is precisely that of the tin trade. And legend, indeed, has made of Joseph of Arimathea a tin merchant, even going so far as to say that, during the "lost" years of Christ, Jesus came as a boy with Joseph to Cornwall and that Jesus taught Joseph how to extract the tin and to purge it of its wolfram. This is the story invoked by Blake in his famous lines, "And did those feet in ancient time walk upon England's mountains green."[10]

Whatever the truth of these stories, Glastonbury is a plausible first site — scholars see it as constituting an early trading centre, situated conveniently, of easy access to the Bristol Channel and sufficiently inland to deter sea raiders. Poetry and science thus do not contradict each other.

The next "problem" to be considered in this attempt to understand the roots of Celtic faith and practice is that of St Patrick. Patrick was born in Britain — either Wales or Scotland — in about AD 387. His was a Christian family, in a period when Christianity was already in decline. His father was a deacon, his grandfather a priest, but Patrick himself seems to have received little formal religious instruction, though clearly Christian ideas must already have formed the unconscious foundations of his thinking. When he was about sixteen, he was snatched from his father's farmstead by Irish raiders and carried off into Ireland as a slave. Here he remained six years, spending his captivity as a shepherd, a lonely occupation which built upon his unformed faith, empowering his vision and his way. Patrick wrote in his *Confession*:

> But after I came to Ireland, and so tended sheep
> every day and often prayed in the daytime, the
> love of God and the fear of Him came to me more
> and more, and faith increased and my spirit was
> stirred, so that in one day I used to say up to a
> hundred prayers and at night nearly as many, and
> I stayed in the forests and on the mountain, and
> before daylight I used to be roused to prayer in
> snow and frost and rain, and felt no harm, nor was
> there any inclination to take things easily in me,
> because, as I see it now, the spirit seethed in me.
> And without a doubt on a certain night I heard in
> my sleep a voice saying to me: You are fasting
> well, and you are very soon going to your
> fatherland. And again, very soon afterwards I heard

the response saying to me: Look your ship is ready! And it was not nearby but about two hundred thousand paces away, and I have never been there nor did I know anyone among the people; and soon afterwards I turned away from that place in flight, and left the man with whom I had been six years and came in the strength of God, who set me on the straight road for my benefit; and I was afraid of nothing until I reached that ship.[11]

Where the ship landed is a moot point. It was either Britain or Gaul. If it was Gaul, then a history is reconstructible for Patrick which is attractive because it puts him into contact with the various streams of Christian life in Europe at that time — particularly the beginnings of monasticism. St Martin had established Ligugé in 360; Cassian, St Victor around 400; and St Honoratus Lérins, where in fact Patrick is supposed to have gone, at about the same time. These latter, and one could also add St Ninian, at Candida Casa in Scotland, brought the Egyptian ideal, "the light from the east," to the west. And since the Celtic Church in so many ways reflects and echoes Egypt and Palestine, it is tempting to see St Patrick at Lérins, that "earthly paradise," perched like so many Irish monasteries on a small island in the sea. To get a sense of the purpose of these — for such earthly paradises would finally be the bases of the Celtic heritage, of the life of prayer, work and fasting established there — the words of Faustus of Riez, himself a Briton or an Irishman and a semi-Pelagian, are evocative:

"It is not for quiet and security," he told the brothers, "that we have formed a community in the monastery, but for a struggle and a conflict. We have met here for a contest, we have embarked upon a war against our sins. . . . The struggle upon which we are engaged is full of hardships, full of dangers, for it is the struggle of man against himself. . . . For this purpose we have gathered together in this tranquil retreat, this spiritual camp, that we may day after day wage an unwearying war against our passions. . . ."[12]

In 432 — which is a traditional cosmological number and synchronizes with the Council of Ephesus that declared Mary *Theotokos*, Mother of God — Patrick was sent as bishop into Ireland. Now, he was the second bishop to be so sent — the first was Palladius — and both were sent, firstly, because the Christians in Ireland must have needed, or even requested, a bishop; and secondly, because there was a fear abroad concerning the Pelagian heresy. Ireland would probably have come up immediately in this connection. Pelagius, after all, was Morgan, a Welshman; he was the first English Christian to write a book, his *Commentary on Romans*; and the Irish always provided, as did the Orthodox east, something of a refuge for Pelagianism in its semi-Pelagian form. This is not to say that the Irish were Pelagians; they were in many ways Augustinian. However, they would have agreed with Pelagius that, "since perfection is possible for man, it is obligatory." But they would not have agreed that human free will could accomplish perfection unaided, or that there was no such thing as original, inherited sin. As with the Eastern Church, the Irish believed in a healthy interdependence of nature and grace.

Ireland, we must never forget, was rural, in an almost absolute sense. There were no villages even. Ireland was still a country of isolated holdings, organized in a tribal, familial culture — kinship binding these holdings together. Most importantly, and implicit in the above,

Irish society was aristocratic, a hierarchical system of individual, autonomous units. There was no state, or nation, or king over all. There were, however, kings, tribal chieftains; and under them warriors and as their equals, "men of special gifts," the *aes-dana* — druids, bards, doctors, historians (for the most part in one) — and finally there were ordinary freedmen. We must understand exactly what all this means. It means amongst other things that just as no single nation or state confronted Patrick, neither did any body of law. Instead of laws there was simply tradition, coupled with the enormous prestige enjoyed by the *aes-dana*. From this we may infer that, though the society was an oral one, it nevertheless by any standards embodied a "high" culture.[13] There were schools, and a great body of traditional knowledge and lore. As Ludwig Bieler commented: "Ireland is unique in the medieval western world in having not only a native literature but also a native tradition of professional learning."[14] Thus, once having acquired a written script, the Irish were culturally well prepared to preserve not only their own traditions, but those of classical Greek and Latin literature also. This they did, thereby ensuring the continuity of European culture.

Patrick's main work, of course, was that of conversion, establishing bishops, churches and the seeds of monasticism. His success in this seems to have resided in his willingness to accept the indigenous traditions and conform his teaching to them. This respect and conformity the receiving wisdom then reciprocated. Two pointers may be given. The first is the story of the conversion in Connaught of the daughters of the High King of Tara. When these questioned him as to who the New God was, and where he dwelt, Patrick replied:

Our God is the God of all men, the God of Heaven
and Earth, of sea and river, of sun and moon and
stars, of the lofty mountain and the lowly valley,
the God above Heaven, the God in Heaven, the
God under Heaven; He has his dwelling round
Heaven and Earth and sea and all that in them is.
He inspires all, he quickens all, he dominates all,
he sustains all. He lights the light of the sun; he
furnishes the light of the light; he has put springs
in the dry land and has set stars to minister to the
greater lights. . . .[15]

In these words of St Patrick has been seen an epitome
of the Celtic monk's holy embrace of nature, his sense
of "ecology." In them we may catch, as H. J.
Massingham said, "a gleam of the new philosophy of
heaven and earth in interdependence and interaction,
formulated by a culture in vital contact with the ancient
nature-worship. . . ."[16] And it is true: everywhere in
Celtic Ireland we will find a holy intimacy of human,
natural and divine. In hermitages and monasteries, on
rocky promontories and lonely hillsides, we find everywhere a tremendous proximity of the human and divine
in nature, an abandonment to spiritual work and simul-
taneously a cultivation of the earth. There is at once a
unique passion for the wild and elemental "as though
to break through the crust of artificial convention to
the very roots of sheer being," coupled with a gentle
human love for all creation, fellow creatures all with
God.

The other piece of Patrick that is indicative, I think,
is his Hymn, the *Deer's Cry*, the *Lorica* or *Breastplate*:
"a corselet for the protection of body and soul." In this,
St Patrick invokes "The Trinity, Three in One, the
Creator of the Universe" and binds to himself its
virtues: those of the Incarnation, Death, Resurrection

and Second Coming; of cherubim, angels, archangels; prayers, predictions, preachings, faiths, deeds; the splendour of fire, the brightness of snow, the speed of lightning, swiftness of wind, depth of sea, stability of earth, compactness of rock. Relying on God, all in all, might, wisdom, ear, word, hand, way, shield, host. Patrick comes finally to Christ — with him, before him, behind him, within him, at his right, at his left, in his lying, in his sitting, in his rising. What is indicative here is the sense of the Trinity as all in all, that the fundamental fact of existence is Unity in Trinity. Trinity in Unity, in Christ. As an old Irish poem puts it:

> O king of kings!
> O sheltering wings, O guardian
>   tree!
> All, all of me,
> Thou Virgin's nurseling, rests in
>   thee.[17]

In any event, Patrick seems to have established a church in perfect conformity with the spirituality of the place. The Druids, Bards, being converted, learnt Latin and incorporated their own traditions into the existing Christian ones. They had always cultivated the "lore of high places," *dindshenchas*. Like all aristocratic societies they had set great store on memory, learning, genealogy. Thus the bards, the *fili*, now became *fer comgne*, synchronizers. Just as Eusebius had composed his Chronicle showing how the great world Kingdoms of Assyria, Egypt, Palestine and Greece had prepared for Christ, now the *fer comgne* prepared their column, showing how all Irish history, from the creation, fitted the same pattern. Indeed, by the seventh century as Robin Flower notes, "the monks had accepted the pagan tradition and put it on one level with the historical material which came to them under the sanction of the fathers of the Church."[18]

This work of compilation, and spiritual investigation, was carried out in the monasteries. The primary purpose of these, of course — with which more "scholarly" activity was not seen to conflict — was contemplation and the practice of the presence of God. "Live in Christ, that Christ may live in you." Columbanus told his students: "Taste and see, how lovely, how pleasant is the Lord." Continuous prayer was thus the ideal, to "pray in every position." A gloss asks, "What is prayer without ceasing?" and it replies: "The answer is not difficult. Some say it is celebrating the canonical hours, but that is not the true meaning. It is when all the members of the body are inclined to good deeds and evil deeds are put away from them. . . ."[19]

Though ascetic, then, the Irish monks were hostile to neither learning nor nature and practised greatly the contemplation of both of these. Indeed, these two — Scripture and nature — were according to Erigena the two shoes of Christ, whose latchet John the Baptist was not yet ready to undo.[20]

As for nature, a gloss says: "Not less does the disposition of the elements set forth concerning God and manifest Him than though it were a teacher who set forth and preached it with his lips." Another proclaims: "The elements sound and show forth the knowledge of God through the work that they do and the alteration that is on them."[21] This is a sacramental universe, birds, beasts and natural phenomena being the signs of a supernatural grace. Indeed, as one reads the monks' stories and poems, birds, beasts and angels blend in a continuous polyphony of revelation. Two short poems may be quoted to illustrate:

Learned in music sings the lark,
I leave my cell to listen;
His open beak spills music, hark!
Where Heaven's bright cloudlets
  glisten.
And so I'll sing my morning psalm
That God bright Heaven may
  give me,
And keep me in eternal calm
And from all sin relieve me.[22]

And again:

Over my head the woodland wall
Rises; the ousel sings to me;
Above my booklet lined for words
The woodland birds shake out
  their glee.
That's the blithe cuckoo chanting
  clear
In mantle grey from bough to
  bough!
God keep me still! for here I write
A scripture bright in great woods
  now.[25]

As Robin Flower says:

It was not only that these scribes and anchorites
lived by the destiny of their dedication in an
environment of wood and sea; it was because they
brought into that environment an eye washed
miraculously clear by continuous spiritual exercise
that they, first in Europe, had that strange vision
of natural things in an almost unnatural purity.[24]

Prayer, then, was the natural accompaniment of the
cultivation of earth and mind. The monasteries were
estates, small farms with livestock and fields. They were

publishing houses, with scriptoria; and finally they were schools. Here the Seven Liberal Arts were practised while the rest of Europe was still in the "dark ages" of transition; the Trivium of grammar, rhetoric and logic (which in practice meant Latin and Greek) and the Quadrivium of arithmetic, geometry, astronomy and music. These, however, were not ends in themselves, but were merely the preliminaries and prerequisites for the study of Scripture and theology. "What is best in the world?" asked Columbanus, author of the most severe and ascetical Rule, and answered:

To do the will of its maker. What is this will? That we should do what he has ordered, that is, that we should live in righteousness and seek devotedly what is eternal. How do we arrive at this? By study. We must therefore study devotedly and righteously. What is our best help in maintaining this study? The Intellectus, which probes everything and, finding none of the world's goods in which it can permanently rest, is converted by reason into the one good which is eternal.[25]

Thus the monasteries assimilated and superseded the ancient bardic and druidic foundations: Bangor, Clonfert, Lismore, Clonmacnoise, Inishmore — such are the names to conjure with. Padraic Pearse wrote of these schools:

It seems to me that there has been nothing nobler in the history of education than this development of the old Irish plan of fosterage under a Christian rule, when to the pagan ideals of strength and truth there were added the Christian ideals of love and humility. And this, remember, was not the education system of an aristocracy, but the education system of a people. It was more democratic than any educational system in the

23

world today. At Clonard Kieran, the son of a carpenter, sat in the same class as Columcille, son of a king. To Clonard or to Aran or to Clonmacnoise went every man, rich or poor, prince or peasant, who wanted to sit at Finian's or at Enda's or at Kieran's feet and to learn of his wisdom.[26]

Generally speaking, the theology accepted and practised was that of the Catholic Church — with an unusual emphasis on Scripture (so that any work could only really be a commentary thereon) and asceticism. The doctrine of God was fully Trinitarian and mystical. Creation was *ex nihilo*, by fiat, through Christ: a theophany with a purpose — that the character of God might be revealed, contemplated, enjoyed, embodied, fulfilled. But with human disobedience, creation had fallen apart from God; and not until Christ's material blood was shed was the original purpose possible again. Now, however, if obedient, creation could become immortal once more. For this, the body was the vehicle. As Secundinus wrote in his Hymn to Patrick: "Flesh he hath prepared as a temple for the Holy Spirit: by whom, in pure activities, it is continually possessed; and he doth offer it to God as a living and acceptable sacrifice."[27]

But there were differences, of course, between the Roman Church and the Celtic Church. There was the question of Easter. The Celtic Church, claiming the authority of St John, used a form of calculation based upon the Jewish lunar calendar which allowed Easter to fall, as did the Passover, in the month of Nisan (March-April). The first Easter had been on the fourteenth day of Nisan. Using their calculation, the Celts celebrated it on the Sunday falling between the fourteenth and twentieth days after the first full moon following the spring equinox. They would do this even if Easter, so calculated, fell on the same day as the Passover, and used an eighty-four year cycle probably inherited from the Council of Arles in 314. The Roman Church made sure Easter never fell on the same day as the Passover, used a solar calendar and had arrived at a different form of cyclical calculation. The Irish were therefore the odd men out, as they were also in the matter of tonsure. The Romans had adopted the tonsure of St Peter, which left a circle, symbolic of the crown of thorns, around the top of the head. The Irish, however, used what they took to be the tonsure of St John, from ear to ear, which their opponents called the tonsure of Simon Magus, perhaps because it was associated with the Druids who were, in Latin, called Magi. Then there were differences in baptism and rites of episcopal confirmation, but all these, though of symbolical importance, were not what really counted.

The overall ethos, which was reflected in organizational habits arising from the tribal background, was the true bone of contention. These made the Celtic Church independent, threatening the growing organizational power of the Romans. In Ireland the spiritual adviser or soul friend (*anmchara*) was primary, rather than the ecclesiastical authority of the bishops. The episcopal structure was threatened further by the fact that, though the bishops still held all ecclesiastical jurisdiction, the actual power lay with the abbots. The abbot, in fact, tended to be the tribal chief, and the tribal structure meant furthermore that the lineage of a monastery would be passed down along kinship lines, following the family which had made the initial grant. Connected to this, Irish monasteries had a large lay, and non-celibate, family population attached to them and, to begin with at least, a monastic female population.

Most important, however, was the fact that these habits gave extreme autonomy and individuality to each foundation: they were more like Zen monasteries, one-pope Churches. Rites, customs and so forth differed locally, and there was no central organization. And, of course, when it came down to it, it was this lack of organization that cost the Celtic Church its power.

The mere century or so following the arrival of St Patrick constitutes the Golden Age of Celtic spirituality. This is the period of the great schools and saints in Ireland, and the beginning of the "pilgrimages for Christ" which were to sow the seeds of the culture of the Middle Ages in Europe. As Jonas tells us in his *Life of Columbanus*:

> After Columbanus had passed many years in
> Bangor, the desire to go into exile began to grow
> in him, for he remembered the words of God to
> Abraham: "Go forth out of thy country and from
> thy kindred, and out of thy father's house, and
> come into the land which I shall show thee."[28]

This was "white martyrdom" when a man for God's sake parted from everything he loved, and suffered and fasted thereby. Thus came into being the *consuetudo peregrinandi*. Many were the schools and monasteries these wanderers founded, the souls they saved, the kings they influenced, the beasts and birds they befriended, the poems they wrote. And the greatest of these — or at least the best loved of these — is St Columba or Columcille.

Columba was born in 521, in Donegal, probably on December 7, a Thursday, for tradition holds Thursday to be the day of Columba. His father was the local chieftain, his grandmother the daughter of King Erc, his mother the daughter of the ruling house of Leinster. Columba was thus of royal blood, and it is always said

26

that he could have been King of Ireland. But he was great in other ways also; Patrick had prophesied his coming while baptizing a chieftain of his tribe:

A manchild shall be born of his family,
He will be a sage, a prophet, a poet,
A loveable lamp, pure, clear.
Who will not utter falsehood.
He will be a sage, he will be pious,
He will be King of the royal graces,
He will be lasting, and will be ever good,
He will be in the eternal Kingdom for his
consolation.[29]

And just before he was born, his mother was visited by an angel bearing a beautiful coloured mantle; she took it from him, but the angel took it back, and it seemed to expand until it crossed and covered valleys, mountains and even seas. Columba's mother was sad at losing such a gift, but the angel comforted her, saying she would have a son who would "blossom for heaven and lead innumerable souls into heaven's own country."

After studying reading and writing with a local teacher, Columba went to Finian, at Molville, one of the masters of Scripture and the saintly life at that time; thence to Gemman, Bard of Leinster, master of the ancient ways. Indeed, in his youth, Columba was as much poet as monk. But then he travelled to Clonard on the Boyne. Here he was ordained and straightway returned to the wilds of Donegal, consumed by one idea, to found a monastery. This he did in 545, at Derry: prayer, fasting, charity, agriculture were the order of the day. But Columba realized that the times required something more. He began to travel, preaching, healing, teaching and founding churches —

about three hundred are ascribed to him. And so he continued until his fortieth year took him across the sea to Scotland.

Why exactly he went is unknown. One tradition is as follows: Columba was a great scribe and lover of sacred writing. Finian of Moville, returning from Italy, brought with him a rare and beautiful book — perhaps a manuscript of Jerome — and kept it to himself. However, finally Columba managed to obtain permission to read it — and not only read it, but surreptitiously made a copy. When Finian found out about this, he demanded the copy as his by right. But Columba refused to comply. Thereupon, Diarmait, King of Meath, ruled: "To every cow her calf, to every book its copy." But Columba still would not return the copy he had made and war broke out. The men of Ulster slew three thousand men of Meath at the Battle of Cooldrevny. Columba was heart-struck, repented and in penance swore never to set foot on Irish soil again.

This story is to be doubted. Columba was everywhere revered. Adamnan simply says: "Being desirous to make a journey for Christ from Ireland into Britain, he sailed forth."[30] *Peregrinari pro Christi*. It was the highest to which a man could aspire.

So Columba came to Iona, "the mecca of the Gael in spiritual geography," as Fiona McLeod says, adding: "To tell the story of Iona is to go back to God and to end in God."[31] Iona is a small, soft, green island — about three and a half miles long — with a hill, some cliffs and a pebbly beach, off the island of Mull on the northwest coast of Scotland. Though small in fact, it is in legend one of the largest of places. "Behold Iona, a blessing on each eye that sees it," says Columba.

Columba arrived on Iona on the eve of Whitsun in

28

563 with twelve companions. His first act on landing was to climb to high ground to make sure that Ireland was no longer visible. Seeing that it was not, the monks then dug a deep tomb and buried their coracle. The name Iona may mean either the Isle of Saints or the Isle of John. Geologically, it is one of the most ancient pieces of rock in the world. Upon this rock Columba and the twelve built their monastery, church and guest-house, and set about cultivating the earth. The fame of the place grew, and soon Columba's family contained upwards of 150 souls. These were of three ranks: the seniors, who transcribed, chiefly, and studied; the working brethren, who tilled the fields and took care of the animals; and the juniors, who were still on probation. There was no personal property, and humility and compassion were continuously exercised in both human and natural companionship. From here, the brothers set out on mission and on retreat; from here Columba himself effected the conversion of the Picts and had his famous contests with the Druids.[32]

Adamnan's *Life of Columba* — one of the greatest of hagiographical works — is written in three sections: prophecies, miracles and visions. The first shows Columba as a person of knowledge; the second as a person of power; the third, epitomizing the first two, as a person of God. Here Columba is shown living in the Spirit of God, in close communion with angels, radiating a divine, immaterial light. Often the other monks would surprise Columba alone at his prayers and discover to their fear and awe the whole structure of the church filled with a celestial light, "descending from the utmost height of heaven, filling all space." Angels were often seen hovering about him, whispering in his ear. And a column of light was sometimes noticed to rise flaming from his head. These are things that

29

seem strange to us today, but they certainly would not
have seemed so to saints of other times and places —
St Symeon the New Theologian, for instance, or St
Seraphim of Sarov. Nor in Celtic tradition is Columba
unique in this. It is related of Fintan for instance that:

A certain brother one night hearing that the holy
father Fintan was keeping vigil in prayer desired
to know in what place he so prayed. And seeking
him on this side and on that, he came into the
burial place of the holy ones. It was a night of
darkness; and the brother gazing at him face to
face saw about him an exceeding light spreading
far, so that his eyes were almost blinded, but God
by the·grace of the Holy Fintan preserved him.[33]

The most perfect story of Columba, however, is the
telling of his death. Columba knew he was to die, and
he knew when. And on the day that he was to die, he
told the brothers he was about to leave them, and then
went out onto the road to return to the monastery,
stopping to rest halfway back:

And while the Saint, feeble with age, as I said
before, sat down for a little while and rested in
that place, behold! there comes up to him the white
horse, that faithful servant, mark you, that used
to carry the milk-pails between the cow-pasture
and the monastery. This creature then coming up
to the Saint, wonderful to say, putting its head in
his bosom, as I believe under the inspiration of
God, in Whose sight every animal is endowed with
a sense of things, because the Creator Himself
hath so ordered it; knowing that his master would
soon depart from him, and that he would see his
face no more, began to utter plaintive moans, and,
as if a man, to shed tears in abundance into the
Saint's lap, and so to weep, frothing greatly. Which

when the attendant saw, he began to drive away that weeping mourner; but the Saint forbad him, saying, "Let him alone! As he loves me so, let him alone; that into this my bosom he may pour out the tears of his most bitter lamentation. Behold! thou, even seeing that thou art a man, and hast a rational soul, couldest in no way know anything about my departure, except what I myself have lately shown to thee; but to this brute animal, destitute of reason, in what way soever the Maker Himself hath willed, He hath revealed that his master is about to go away from him." And, so saying, he blessed his sorrowing servant the horse, then turning about to go away from him.

Columba then went and blessed the Island; blessed the granary; blessed the animals, blessed the monks and passed away, by the altar:

Then, in the next place, in the middle of the night, at the sound of the ringing of the bell, he rises in haste and goes to the church; and, running more quickly than the rest, he enters alone, and on bended knees falls down in prayer beside the altar. Diormit his attendant, following more slowly, at the same moment sees from a distance that the whole church is filled within, in the direction of the Saint, with angelic light. But when he approaches the door, the same light that he has seen, which was also seen by a few other of the brethren, as they were standing at a distance, quickly disappeared. So Diormit, entering the church keeps on asking, in a lamentable voice, "Where art thou, father?" And feeling his way through the darkness, the lights of the brethren not yet being brought in, he finds the Saint prostrate before the altar; and, lifting him up a

little and sitting beside him, he placed the holy
head in his bosom. And meanwhile, the
congregation of monks running up with the lights,
and seeing their father dying, began to weep.
And, as we have learnt from some who were there
present, the Saint, his soul not yet departing, with
his eyes opened upward, looked about on either
hand with a wonderful cheerfulness and joy of
countenance; doubtless seeing the holy angels
coming to meet him. Then Diormit lifts up the
holy right hand of the Saint so that he may bless
the choir of monks. But also the venerable man
himself, so far as he could, at the same time moved
his hand, so that, mark you, he might still be
seen, while passing away, to bless the brethren by
the motion of his hand, though he was not able
to do so with his voice. And, after his holy
benediction thus expressed, he immediately
breathed out his spirit. Which having left the
tabernacle of the body, his face remained ruddy,
and wonderfully gladdened by an angelic vision;
so that it appeared not to be that of one dead, but
of one living and sleeping. Meanwhile, the whole
church resounded with mournful lamentations.[34]

By this time, however, the story was already into its
next chapter and the Celtic seed had moved closer to
its European germination. For by the kind offices of
Saint and King Oswald of Northumbria, Aidan was
already about to depart to establish Celtic Christianity
in England, at Lindisfarne in Northumbria. There is a
slight time lag, in fact, but not much. In the years
immediately following the death of Columba, Oswald,
exiled from his kingdom, sought refuge on Iona. When
he was finally able to return to Northumbria, therefore,
his first act was to send to Iona for a bishop. Corman

came first, but he was too hard; so Aidan went, a gentle, beautiful figure, who knew how to feed beginners on the milk of doctrine. Aidan in a way is the last pure Celt: his successors were already part of the Roman-European venture.

Aidan died in 651; and on the day of his death a young boy herding sheep on a lonely hillside had a vision of a great stream of light breaking through the sky, and a choir of angels descending and gathering up a soul of exquisite brightness. The boy was Cuthbert. Cuthbert, in fact, was the first Roman Bishop of Lindisfarne, presiding over the monastery in the period of adjustment following the Synod of Whitby. Though he took little part in ecclesiastical disputes, his position seems to have been that the unity of the Church was primary.

Cuthbert, then, in many ways is a transitional figure, but in his love of solitude and nature he is Celtic. Once at Coldingham, after having preached to the nuns there, he retired to the beach to pray. A curious monk followed him to see what he did. He saw Cuthbert, his arms uplifted, walk into the icy water until the waves broke under his armpits. In this way he spent the night in prayer and meditation; at dawn, he emerged from the water and fell upon his knees on the sand. Two small sea otters tumbled and played around his legs. Then, his prayers finished, Cuthbert joyfully blessed the otters, who scurried back into the water again.[35]

Thus, as a sensible, historical unit the Celtic Church was not long in existence. St Augustine, the missionary from Rome, landed the year Columba died, AD 597. By 664 and the Synod of Whitby, the Celtic Church as a visible entity was over. But this is not to say that its work was done. In a sense it was only just beginning. Heiric of Auxerre exclaimed in 870, "Almost all Ireland, despising the sea, is migrating to our shores with a herd of philosophers." Decade after decade the stream of learned immigrants continued, bringing with them "divine and human wisdom." The kings and chieftains of Europe loved these peregrini; they were as welcome at court as at church or in the monastery. Their habits of thought in science, music, literature, as well as theology, were to have far-reaching and profound effects. Alcuin and John Scotus Erigena are only the brightest of these lights and the lesser lights were probably equally effective in the immediate transformation of European culture. "If anyone desires wisdom, we have it to sell," announced two peregrini arriving at the court of Charlemagne, who called them into his presence and inquired the price of their wisdom. The two's answer was "suitable places and ready students, and food and clothing without which our peregrination cannot continue." These two are described as "incomparably erudite both in secular matters and in Holy Scripture."[36] In both of these, indeed, the Celtic heritage formed the Golden Age of Europe — monasteries, cathedrals, universities — upon whose riches we all still feed.

References

1 Chadwick, Nora, *Age of the Saints in the Celtic Church*, p. 2.
2 Massingham, H. J. *Tree of Life*, p. 40.
3 Taylor, John W. *Coming of the Saints*.
4 Wyatt, Isobel, "Goddess into Saint".
5 Yeats, W. B. *Collected Poems*, p. 450.
6 Wyatt, Isobel, "Goddess into Saint".
7 Curtayne, Alice, *St Brigit of Ireland*.
8 Taylor, John W. *Coming of the Saints*, p. 176.
9 Taylor, John W. *Coming of the Saints*, pp. 201f.
10 Taylor, John W. *Coming of the Saints*, pp. 173–233.
11 Marsh, A. *St Patrick and his Writings*, p. 27.
12 Ryan, John, *Irish Monasticism*.
13 Dillon, Miles (Ed.) *Early Irish Society*.
14 Bieler, Ludwig, "The Island of Scholars" p. 213.
15 Massingham, H. J. *Tree of Life*. p. 37.
16 Massingham, H. J. *Tree of Life*, p. 37.
17 Flower, Robin, *Irish Tradition*, p. 47.
18 Flower, Robin, *Irish Tradition*, p. 5.
19 Hardinge, Leslie, *Celtic Church in Britain*, p. 67.
20 Erigena, John Scotus, *Homily*.
21 Hardinge, Leslie, *Celtic Church in Britain*, pp. 59f.
22 Flower, Robin, *Irish Tradition*, p. 54.
23 Flower, Robin, *Irish Tradition*, p. 42.
24 Flower, Robin, *Irish Tradition*, p. 42.
25 Ryan, John, *Irish Monasticism*.
26 Quoted in Katherine Sherman, *Flowering of Ireland*, p. 107.
27 Harney, Martin, *Legacy of Saint Patrick*, p. 136.
28 Wilson, J. *Life of Columba*, p. 15.
29 Menzies, Lucie, *Saint Columba of Iona*, pp. 1f.
30 Adamnan, *Prophecies of St Columba*, p. 4.
31 Macleod Fiona, *Divine Adventure: Iona*, pp. 93f.
32 Menzies, Lucie, *Saint Columba of Iona*, pp. 81–99.
33 Flower, Robin, *Irish Tradition*, p. 56.
34 Adamnan, *Prophecies of St Columba*, pp. 133–36.
35 Stranks, C. J. *Life and Death of St Cuthbert*.
36 McNeill, John, *Celtic Churches*. pp. 178, 180.

Full details of the publications are given in the Bibliography, p. 141.

An anthology of Celtic Christianity

*Edited by William Parker Marsh
with Christopher Bamford*

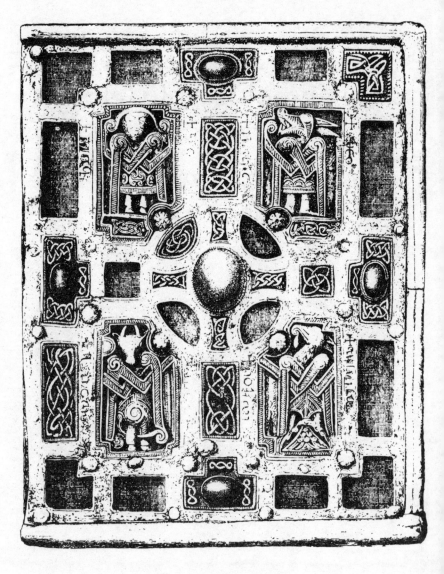

Case of Molaisse's Gospels

God's Aid

God to enfold me,
  God to surround me,
God in my speaking,
  God in my thinking.

God in my sleeping,
  God in my waking,
God in my watching,
  God in my hoping.

God in my life,
  God in my lips,
God in my soul,
  God in my heart.

God in my sufficing,
  God in my slumber,
God in mine ever-living soul,
  God in mine eternity.

Carmina Gadelica

Invocation

Son of the Dawn
Son of the clouds
Son of the stars
Son of the elements
Son of the heavens
Son of the Moon
Son of the Sun.

Of the Situation of Ireland

Ireland, in breadth, and for wholesomeness and serenity of climate, far surpasses Britain; for the snow scarcely ever lies there above three days: no man makes hay in the summer for winter's provision, or builds stables for his beasts of burden. No reptiles are found there, and no snake can live there; for though often carried thither out of Britain, as soon as the ship comes near the shore, and the scent of the air reaches them, they die. On the contrary, almost all things in the island are good against poison. In short, we have known that when some persons have been bitten by serpents, the scrapings of leaves of books that were brought out of Ireland, being put into water, and given them to drink, have immediately expelled the spreading poison and assuaged the swelling. The island abounds in milk and honey, nor is there any want of vines, fish, or fowl; and it is remarkable for deer and goats.

The Venerable Bede

Patrick's Vision of Ireland

I saw in a vision of the night a man whose name was Victoricus coming as it were from Ireland with countless letters. He gave me one of them, and I read the beginning of the letter, which was entitled "The Voice of the Irish." And whilst I was reading aloud the beginning of the letter I thought that at that very moment I heard the voices of those who dwelt beside the Wood of Foclut, which is nigh unto the Western Sea. And

41

thus they cried, as with one mouth, "We beseech thee, holy youth, to come and walk once more amongst us."

And I was exceedingly touched in my heart, and could read no more, and so I awoke. Thanks be to God, after many years the Lord granted to them according to their earnest cry.

Confession of Saint Patrick

Patrick's Blessing on Munster

Blessing on the men of Munster,
Men, boys, women!
Blessing on the land
That gives them fruit.

Blessing on every treasure
That shall be produced on their plains,
Without any one in want of help,
God's blessing on Munster!

Blessing on their peaks,
On their bare flagstones,
Blessing on their glens,
Blessing on their ridges.

Like sand of sea under ships,
Be the number of their hearths:
On slopes, on plains,
On mountains, on peaks.

Translated by Whitley Stokes

Patrick and the Druids

When Patrick knew that unto him God had granted the apostleship of Ireland, he went to Rome to have ecclesiastical orders given him; and Celestinus, Abbot of Rome, read orders over him, Germanus and Amatho, king of the Romans, being present with them. Then too was the name "Patricus" given unto him, a name of power as the Romans think, to wit, one who looseth hostages. He, then, loosed the hostageship and slavery of the Gael to the Devil. And when the orders were a-reading out, three choirs mutually responded, namely, the choir of the children from the wood of Fochlad. This is what all sang: "All we Irish beseech thee, holy Patrick, to come and walk among us and free us."

At that time there was a certain fierce heathen king in Ireland, namely Loegaire son of Niall, and in Tara were his residence and his royal grip. In the fifth year of his reign, Patrick came to Ireland. Loegaire had wizards who used to foretell by their wizardry what was before them. Lochru and Lucatmael were the chiefs of them, and they were the authors of that art of false prophecy. They foretold that an evil-lawed prophet would come over sea to their land and teach, and that a multitude would receive him, and that he would find love and reverence with the men of Ireland, and that he would cast the kings and the lords out of their realm, and would destroy all the images of the idols, and that the usage which would come there would abide in Ireland for ever and ever.

Two years or three years before Patrick's arrival, this is what they used to prophesy:

Adzehead* will come over a furious sea;
His mantle head-holed, his staff crook-headed,
His dish [altar] in the east of his house.
All his household shall answer
Amen, Amen!

Now, when Patrick had completed his voyage and brought his vessels to land in Ireland, the high-tide of Easter drew nigh. Patrick thought that there was no place fitter for celebrating this chief solemnity of the year than in Mag Breg, in the place wherein was the chief abode of the idolatry and wizardry of Ireland, to wit, in Tara. Then he and his companions anchored their vessel in Inver Colptha and went along the land until they came to Ferta Fer Feicc [the Graves of Fiacc's Men], and Patrick's tent was pitched in that place, and he struck the paschal fire. It happened that that was the time at which was celebrated the high-tide of the heathen, to wit, the feast of Tara. The kings and the lords and the chiefs used to come to Tara, to Loegaire son of Niall, to celebrate the festival therein. The wizards, also, and the augurs would come so that they were prophesying to them. On that night, then, the fire of every hearth in Ireland was quenched, and it was proclaimed by the King that no fire should be kindled in Ireland before the fire of Tara. Patrick knew not that, and even though he had known, this would not have hindered him.

As the folk of Tara were biding there, they saw at some distance from them the paschal consecrated fire which Patrick had kindled. It lighted up the whole of

* Patrick, so-called from his tonsure.

44

Mag Breg. Then said the King: "That is a breach of a ban and law of mine. Find out who hath done so."

"We see," said the wizards, "the fire, and we know that unless it is quenched on the night on which it was made, it will not be quenched till doomsday. He, moreover, who kindles it will vanquish the kings and lords of Ireland unless he is forbidden."

Then the King was mightily disturbed. "This shall not be," saith he. "We will go and slay the man who kindled the fire." Then his chariots and his horses were yoked, and they went at the end of the night to the Graves of Fiacc's Men.

"Thou shouldst take heed," said the wizards, "not to go to the place where the fire was made, that thou mayst not do reverence to the man who kindled it; but stay outside, and let him be called out to thee, that he may judge that thou art the King, and that he is the subject, and we will argue in your presence."

They came thereafter and unyoked their horses and their chariots before the Graves. Patrick was called out to them after they had made a rule that no one should rise up to meet him lest he should believe in him. So Patrick arose and went forth, and saw the chariots and the horses unyoked, whereupon he chanted the prophetic verse: "Some trust in chariots and some in horses; but we in the name of the Lord our mighty God." They were biding before him with the rims of their shields against their chins, and none rose up before him save one man only in whom was a nature from God, namely Erc son of Deg. Patrick bestowed a blessing upon him, and he believed in God and confessed the Catholic faith, and was baptized.

Then came one of the wizards, to wit, Lochru, fiercely and angrily against Patrick, and reviled the Trinity and the Christian faith. Then Patrick cried in a

45

great voice, "Lord, who canst do all things, and on whose power dependeth all that exists, and who hast sent us hither to preach Thy name to the heathen, let this ungodly man who blasphemeth Thy name be lifted up and let him forthwith die!" Swifter than speech, at Patrick's word, the wizard was raised into the air and forthwith again cast down, and he was broken in pieces, and dust and ashes were made of him in the presence of all. The heathen were adread at that.

The King, then, was greatly enraged against Patrick and wished at once to kill him. When Patrick saw the heathen arising against him, he cried with a great voice, and said: "Let God arise, and let His enemies be scattered: let them also that hate Him flee before Him. Like as the smoke vanisheth, so let them vanish; like as wax melteth at the fire, so let the ungodly perish at the presence of God." At once darkness came over the sun, and a great earthquake and trembling of arms took place there. It seemed to them that the sky fell on the earth, and the horses went off in fright, and the wind whirled the chariots through the fields. And each rose up to the other in the assembly, so that each of them was after slaying the other, and fifty men of them fell in that uprising by Patrick's curse.

The heathen fled on every side, so that only three remained, namely, Loegaire and his queen and one of his household and they feared greatly. When terror seized the queen she went to Patrick and said to him "O righteous one and O mighty one, kill not the King, for he shall submit to thee, and give thee thine own will." The King came and gave his will to Patrick by word of mouth, but gave it not from his heart; and he told Patrick to go after him to Tara that he might give him his will before the men of Ireland. That, however, was not what was biding in his mind, but to kill Patrick,

46

for he left ambushes before him on every road from that to Tara. But God permitted not this. Patrick went with eight young clerics and Benen as a gillie with them, and Patrick blessed them before going. A cloak of darkness went over them so that not a man of them appeared. Howbeit, the heathen who were biding in the snares saw eight deer going past them under the mountain, and behind them a fawn with a white bird on its shoulder: that was Patrick with his eight, and Benen behind them with Patrick's writing-tablets on his back. And Patrick sang this hymn, and its name is "The Deer's Cry":*

I arise today
Through a mighty strength, the invocation of the
    Trinity,
Through belief in the threeness,
Through confession of the oneness
Of the Creator of Creation.

I arise today
Through the strength of Christ's birth with His
    baptism,
Through the strength of His crucifixion with His
    burial,
Through the strength of His resurrection with His
    ascension,
Through the strength of His descent for the
    judgment of Doom.

I arise today
Through the strength of the love of Cherubim,
In obedience of angels,
In the service of archangels,

* Translated by Kuno Meyer

47

In hope of resurrection to meet with reward,
In prayers of patriarchs,
In predictions of prophets,
In preachings of apostles,
In faiths of confessors,
In innocence of holy virgins,
In deeds of righteous men.

I arise today
Through the strength of heaven:
Light of sun,
Radiance of moon,
Splendour of fire.
Speed of lightning,
Swiftness of wind,
Depth of sea,
Stability of earth,
Firmness of rock.

I arise today
Through God's strength to pilot me:
God's might to uphold me,
God's wisdom to guide me,
God's eye to look before me,
God's ear to hear me,
God's word to speak for me,
God's hand to guard me,
God's way to lie before me,
God's shield to protect me,
God's host to save me
From snares of devils,
From temptation of vices,
From every one who shall wish me ill,
Afar and anear,
Alone and in a multitude.

I summon today all these powers between me and
    these evils:
Against every cruel, merciless power that may
    oppose my body and soul:
Against incantations of false prophets,
Against black laws of pagandom,
Against false laws of heretics,
Against craft and idolatry,
Against spells of women and smiths and wizards,
Against every knowledge that corrupts man's body
    and soul.

Christ to shield me today
Against poison, against burning,
Against drowning, against wounding,
So that there may come to me abundance of
    reward.
Christ with me, Christ before me, Christ behind
    me,
Christ in me, Christ beneath me, Christ above me,
Christ on my right, Christ on my left,
Christ when I lie down, Christ when I sit down,
    Christ when I arise,
Christ in the heart of every one who thinks of me,
Christ in the mouth of every one who speaks of
    me,
Christ in every eye that sees me
Christ in every ear that hears me.

I arise today
Through a mighty strength, the invocation of the
    Trinity,
Through belief in the threeness,
Through confession of the oneness
Of the Creator of Creation.

Thereafter went Loegaire at daybreak to Tara in grief and in shame, together with the few that had escaped with him.

On the following day the men of Ireland went to Tara to carouse, for with them the feast of Tara was an especial day. When they were carousing and thinking of the conflict they had fought on the day before, they saw Patrick standing still in the middle of Tara, the doors being shut, as when Christ came into the dining room (John 20:26). Because Patrick thought, "I will go that I may manifest my readiness before the men of Ireland. It is not 'a candle under a vat' that I will make of myself. So that I may see who will believe in me, and who will not believe." No one rose up before him in the house save only Dubthach Maccu-Lugair, poet of the island of Ireland and of the King. Patrick bestowed a blessing on him and on his offspring.

Patrick then is summoned to the King's couch that he might consume food and be proven in prophecy. Patrick refused not that because he knew what would come thereof. The wizard Lucatmael went to drink with him because he had a mind to avenge on Patrick what had been done the day before to his comrade, Lochru. So Lucatmael put a sip of poison into the cup that stood at Patrick's hand, so that he might see what he would do unto it. Patrick observed that, and he blessed the cup, and the liquor curdled. He then inverted the vessel, and out of it fell the poison which the wizard had put into it. Patrick again blessed the cup, and the liquor was turned into its proper nature. God's name and Patrick's were magnified thereby. This is what Patrick recited over the cup: "Though we have knowledge of it, though we have not, it shall be quaffed in the name of Jesus Christ."

Then said the King to his gillie Crunnmoel, "Go out

on the causeway of Tara and lay thee down thereon and let them rub dough mixed with blood about thy head, and let them say that it is a fall thou fellest upon the stones so that thou diedst, and I will tell the cleric to come to bring thee to life, and though he tell thee to rise, arise not." Thus was it done. When Patrick saw the body, God made manifest to him that guile was practised on him, wherefore he said:

O my Crunnmoel, O my bald youth, O my hero,
Though thou attainedst one thing, though thou
   hast not attained, thou hast not arisen.
Though thou hast fallen, though thou hast not
   fallen upon the stones — a final deed.
Though thou attainedst a thing, though thou hast
   not attained, thou art not healed.

It is certain then that through Patrick's curse Crunnmoel was not healed, and from that time forth he arose not at all.

Then came the hosts till they were all biding without Tara in the plain. "Let us," said Lucatmael, "work miracles before the host in that great plain."

Said Patrick: "Which be they?"

Said the wizard: "Let us bring snow on the plain till the plain be white in front of us."

Said Patrick to him: "I have no desire to go against God's will."

Said the wizard: "I will bring the snow on the plain although it be not thy desire." Then he began the chants of wizardry and the arts of devilry, so that the snow fell till it reached men's girdles. They all saw and marvelled greatly.

Said Patrick: "We see this. Put it away if thou canst." Said the wizard: "I cannot do that till this hour tomorrow."

"By my God's doom!" saith Patrick, "it is in evil thy

51

power stands, and not in good." Patrick blessed the plain throughout the four quarters. Quicker than speech, at Patrick's word the snow vanished, without rain, without sun, without wind.

Then at the wizard's incantation came darkness over the face of the earth. Thereat the hosts cried out. Said Patrick: "Dispel the darkness."

The wizard said: "I cannot today."

Patrick prayed to the Lord, and blessed the plain, and the darkness was banished and the sun shone, and all gave thanks.

They were for a long while at this contention in the presence of the King. And even as Nero said to Simon (Magus) and to Peter, saith the King to them: "Cast your books into water; and we will honour him whose books shall come out unhurt."

Patrick replied: "I will do so."

And the wizard said: "I am unwilling to go with him to the ordeal of water. For he hath water as a god."

He said this because he had heard that Patrick used to baptize with water.

And the King answered: "Cast them, then, into fire."

And Patrick saith: "I am ready."

But the wizard, unwilling, said: "This man, turn about in alternate years, venerates as a god now water and now fire."

"That will not be done," saith Patrick, "but since thou sayest that I adore a god of fire, thou shalt go, if thou art willing, apart into a house completely shut up, and a cleric of my household before thee, and my chasuble around thee, and thy wizard's tunic round my cleric, and fire shall be put into the house, so that God may deal dooms on you therein." That counsel was settled then by them, that is, by the men of Ireland around Loegaire.

Then came to Patrick three children who were biding in hostageship with Loegaire. They weep to Patrick. Patrick asks, "What is the matter?"

"A prince's troth," say they, "hath been broken in this chief city of the Gael, namely, the house that is a-building as well for the wizard as thy servant, thus is it a-building, half thereof fresh and half dry, the fresh half for the wizard and the dry half for thy servant."

Patrick puts his finger on the right cheek of each of the children, and he puts a tear from the cheek of each child on his left palm, and he breathes under the tears and made three gems thereof. The children swallowed the gems. "Three special gems," said Patrick, "will be born from them," to wit, Columb Cille [Columba] and Comgall and Finnia.

Thereafter the house was built, one side of it dry, the other fresh. Then the wizard was sent into the fresh side, with Patrick's chasuble around him. Then Benen was sent into the dry side with the wizard's tunic around him. So the house was closed around them, and a bar was put on it outside, before the host, and fire is set therein. A mighty marvel came to pass there through Patrick's prayer. The fresh half of the house was burnt and the wizard in the midst of the chasuble, and the fire destroyed not the chasuble in the least. The dry half, however, wherein Benen was biding was not burnt, and Benen was saved in the midst of the wizard's tunic, and the tunic was burnt so that ashes were made thereof.

Terror then seized Leogaire, and he knelt to Patrick and believed in God. And on that day many thousands believed and were baptized.

Adapted from The Tripartite Life of Patrick and The Lebar Brecc Homily on St Patrick

Rune of Saint Patrick

At Tara today in this fateful hour
I place all Heaven with its power,
And the Sun with its brightness,
And the snow with its whiteness,
And Fire with all the strength it hath,
And lightning with its rapid wrath,
And the winds with their swiftness along the path,
And the sea with its deepness,
And the rocks with their steepness,
And the Earth with its starkness:
All these I place
By God's almighty help and grace,
Between myself and the powers of Darkness.

Patrick on Cruachan Aigle

Then Patrick went to Cruachan Aigle* on Saturday of
Whitsuntide. The angel Victor came to commune with
him, and said to him: "God gives thee not what thou
demandest, because it seems to him excessive and obsti-
nate, for great are the requests."

"Is that His pleasure?" said Patrick.

"It is," saith the angel.

"Then this is *my* pleasure," saith Patrick. "I will not

* Now Croagh Patrick, a mountain in Mayo.

go from this Rick till I am dead or till the requests are granted to me."

And for forty days and forty nights Patrick fasted in that place, having four stones about him and a stone under him, even as Moses fasted on Mount Sinai when the Law was delivered unto him. For they, Moses and Patrick, were alike in many ways. To both God spoke out of the fire. Six score years was the age of them both. Each was a leader of people. And the burial-place of each is uncertain.

Now, at the end of those forty days and forty nights, the mountain was filled against him with devils in shapes of black birds, so that he knew not heaven nor earth. He sang maledictive psalms at them, but they left him not because of this. Then his anger grew against them, and he struck his bell at them so that the men of Ireland heard its voice. He then flung his bell at them so that its gap broke out of it, and that is "Brigit's gapling." The devils fled forthwith upon the sea, as far as the eye could reach, and drowned themselves in that place. No devil came to the land of Ireland after that till the end of seven years and seven months and seven days and seven nights.

After the devils fled, there came a great host of angels in shapes of white birds, and sang to the Lord noble music to comfort Patrick. The angel Victor came to console Patrick and saith to him, "Thou shalt bring yon number of souls out of pain, and all that can fill the space which thine eye reaches over the sea."

"That is not a boon to me," saith Patrick, "not far doth mine eye reach over the sea."

"Then thou shall have both sea and land," saith the angel.

"Is there aught else that He granteth to me besides that?" saith Patrick.

"There is," saith the angel. "Seven persons on every Saturday till Doom to be taken out of Hell's pains."

"If He should give aught to me," saith Patrick, "Let my twelve men be given."

"Thou shalt have them," saith the angel, "and now get thee gone from the Rick."

"I will not get me gone," saith Patrick, "since I have been tormented, till I am blessed. Is there aught else that will be given to me?"

"There is," saith the angel. "Thou shalt have of Hell's pains seven every Thursday and twelve every Sunday; and now get thee gone from the Rick."

"I will not get me gone," saith Patrick, "since I have been tormented, till I am blessed. Is there aught else, then, that is granted to me?"

"There is," saith the angel: "a great sea came over Ireland seven years before the Judgment;* and now get thee gone from the Rick."

"I will not get me gone," saith Patrick, "since I have been tormented, till I am blessed."

"Is there aught else that thou wouldst demand?" saith the angel.

"There is," saith Patrick: "that the Saxons should not dwell in Ireland, by consent or perforce, so long as I abide in Heaven."

"Thou shalt have this," saith the angel, "and now get thee gone from the Rick."

"I will not get me gone," saith Patrick, "since I have been tormented, till I am blessed. Is there aught else granted to me?"

"There is," saith the angel: "every one who shall sing thy hymn, from one watch to the other, shall not have pain or torture."

---

* So that Ireland will be saved from the persecution of the Antichrist.

"The hymn is long and difficult," saith Patrick.

"Every one who shall sing it from '*Christus illum*' to the end, and every one who shall give aught in thy name, and every one who shall perform penitence in Ireland, his soul shall not go to Hell; and now get thee gone from the Rick."

"I will not get me gone," saith Patrick, "since I have been tormented, till I am blessed. Is there aught else?"

"There is," saith the angel, "a person for every hair on thy chasuble thou shalt bring out of pains on the day of Doomsday."

"Which of the other saints who labour for God will not bring that number into Heaven? Verily I will not take that," saith Patrick.

"Question, what wilt thou take?" saith the angel.

"Not hard to say," saith Patrick. "Seven persons for every hair that abides on the chasuble to be taken out of Hell on the day of Doomsday."

"Thou shalt have this," saith the angel, "and now get thee gone from the Rick."

"I will not get me gone," saith Patrick.

"Thy hand will be seized," saith the angel.

"Except if the high King of seven heavens should come, I will not get me gone, since I have been tormented, till I am blessed."

"Is there aught else thou wouldst demand?" saith the angel.

"There is," saith Patrick. "On the day that the twelve thrones shall be on the Mount, when the four rivers of fire shall be around the mountain, and the three households shall be there, to wit, the household of Heaven and the household of Earth and the household of Hell, let me myself be judge over the men of Ireland on that day."

"Assuredly," saith the angel, "that is not got from the Lord."

"Unless it is got from Him," saith Patrick, "departure from this Rick shall not be got from me, from today till Doom."

The angel went to Heaven. Patrick went to mass. The angel came back at nones. "How is that?" saith Patrick.

"Thus," saith the angel. "All creatures, visible and invisible, including the twelve apostles, besought the Lord, and they have obtained. The Lord said, 'There hath not come, and there will not come, after the apostles, a man more admirable, were it not for his hardness.' What thou hast prayed for, thou shalt have. Strike thy bell and fall on thy knees, and there will be a consecration of the folk of Ireland, both living and dead."

Saith Patrick: "A blessing on the bountiful King who hath given; and the Rick shall now be departed from."

Adapted from The Tripartite Life of Patrick
and The Lebar Brecc Homily on St. Patrick

Holy Patrick, Full of Grace

When holy Patrick, full of grace,
Suffered on Cruach, that blest place,
In grief and gloom enduring then
For Eire's women, Eire's men.

God for his comfort sent a flight
Of birds angelically bright
That sang above the darkling lake
A song unceasing for his sake.

'Twas thus they chanted, all and some:
'Come hither, Patrick, hither come!
Shield of the Gael, thou light of story,
Appointed star of golden glory!'

Thus singing, all those fair birds smite
The waters with soft wings in flight
Till the dark lake its gloom surrenders
And rolls a tide of silvery splendors.

Translated by Robin Flower

Patrick's Devotion

Now Patrick hath been likened to the Patriarchs: to wit, first he was a true pilgrim, like Abraham; meek, forgiving, like Moses; a psalmist of God's praise was he, like David son of Jesse; a student of wisdom like Solomon; a chosen vessel for proclaiming truth, like apostle Paul; a man full of the grace and favour of the Holy Ghost, like John son of Zebedee; a lion in strength and boldness to bring the sinful and wicked of the world to faith and belief; a serpent in cunning and prudence for noticing every onslaught; a dove, mild and gentle in heart's desire and perfect word and righteous deed; a laborious servant to the Creator as to godliness and humility, and teaching of all good things, as many relate.

Now, this was the rule of his devotion: to wit, he

used to sing all the psalms with their hymns and canticles and apocalypse, and two hundred other prayers every day. He used to baptize, to preach, and to celebrate the canonical hours according to their due order: he used to offer Christ's Body and Blood. He used to make the sign of the cross over his face a hundred times from one canonical hour to another. In the first watch of the night he used to sing a hundred psalms and make two hundred genuflections. In the second watch he used to be in cold water; the third watch in contemplation; the fourth watch on bare clay, with a stone under his head and a wet mantle about him. He used to ordain, anoint, consecrate, and bless. He used to cure lepers, the blind, the lame, the deaf, the dumb, and folk of every disease besides. He used to cast out devils; he used to raise the dead to life.

From The Lebar Brecc Homily on St Patrick

Michael Militant

O Michael Militant,
   Thou king of the angels,
Shield thy people
   With the power of thy sword,
     Shield thy people
     With the power of thy sword.

Spread thy wing
   Over sea and land,
East and west,
   And shield us from the foe,
     East and west,
     And shield us from the foe.

Brighten thy feast
  From heaven above;
Be with us in the pilgrimage
  And in the twistings of the fight;
    Be with us in the pilgrimage
    And in the twistings of the fight.

Thou chief of chiefs,
  Thou chief of the needy,
Be with us in the journey
  And in the gleam of the river;
    Be with us in the journey
    And in the gleam of the river.

Thou chief of chiefs,
  Thou chief of the angels,
Spread thy wing
  Over sea and land,
  For thine is their fullness,
  Thine is their fullness,
    Thine own is their fullness,
    Thine own is their fullness.

Carmina Gadelica

Brigit, the Mary of the Gael

Here is related somewhat of the miracles and marvels of the holy Brigit. There was a man named Dubthach who bought a bondmaid named Broicsech, and she became with child by him. One day thereafter he and the bondmaid along with him went in a chariot past the house of a certain wizard. Upon seeing the bondmaid, the wizard said: "Marvellous will be the child that is in her womb, for the bondmaid will bring forth a daughter conspicuous and radiant, who will shine like a sun among the stars of heaven; her like will not be known on earth."

One morning the bondmaid went at sunrise with a vessel full of milk in her hand, and when she put one of her two footsteps over the threshold, the other foot being inside, then she brought forth the daughter, even Saint Brigit. The maidservants washed the babe with the milk that was still in her mother's hand. That was in accord with Brigit's merit, even with the brightness and sheen of her chastity.

On a certain day the bondmaid went to milk her kine, and left the child alone sleeping in her house. Certain neighbours beheld the house, wherein the girl lay, ablaze, so that one flame was made thereof from earth to heaven. When they came to rescue the house, the fire appeared not, but they said that the girl was full of the grace of the Holy Spirit.

Then the holy virgin was reared till she was a handmaid. And everything to which her hand was set used to increase. She tended the sheep, she satisfied the birds, she fed the poor. One day a noble guest came to the house of Dubthach, and hospitality was shown to him. Five pieces of bacon were given to Brigit to be boiled for him. And a miserable hungry hound came into the house to Brigit. Out of pity Brigit gave him the fifth piece of bacon. The hound was not satisfied with that, so Brigit gave him another piece. She thought the guest was asleep, but this was not so. Then came Dubthach and asked Brigit, "Hast thou boiled the bacon? And do the portions remain?"

"Count them," said she. Dubthach did so, and not one of them was wanting. The guest told Dubthach what Brigit had done. The guests did not consume that food, for they were unworthy thereof; but it was dealt out to the poor and needy.

Once upon a time a certain faithful woman took Brigit with her into Moy Liffey, where a gathering of the synod of Leinster was held. It was manifested to Bishop Ibhair, who was in the assembly, that Mary the Virgin was coming into the assembly. On the next day came the woman, Brigit alone with her, unto the assembly. Then said Bishop Ibhair: "This is the Mary whom I beheld." And the whole host blessed Saint Brigit. Wherefore Brigit was thenceforth called "The Mary of the Gael."

Now, of her father's wealth and property, whatsoever her hands would find or would get, Brigit used to give to the poor and needy of the Lord. Wherefore her father became displeased with her and desired to sell the holy Brigit. He went with her in a chariot, and said: "Not for honour or for reverence to thee art thou carried in the chariot; but to take thee to sell thee, that thou mayst grind at the quern of Dunlaing, son of Enna, king of Leinster."

When they came to the king's fortress, Dubthach

went in, and left his sword near Brigit in the chariot. And a leper came to Brigit, and besought her to bestow something upon him. Brigit handed him her father's sword. Said Dubthach to the king when he had come inside, "Wilt thou buy my daughter from me?"

"Wherefore sellest thou thine own daughter?" said Dunlaing.

"Not hard to say. She is selling my wealth and bestowing it on wretched worthless men."

"Let her be brought to us that we may see her," said Dunlaing.

Dubthach went for her, and when he came to the chariot he saw not his sword. He asked Brigit what she had done with it. "I gave it," said she, "to a poor man who came to beg of me."

Dubthach was mightily enraged with her for having given the sword away. When Brigit came before the king, he said, "Why dost thou steal thy father's property and wealth, and what is worse, why hast thou given the sword away?"

Then said Brigit: "The Virgin's Son knoweth if I had thy power, with all thy wealth, and with all thy Leinster, I would give them all to the Lord of the Elements."

Said the king to Dubthach, "It is not meet for us to deal with this maiden, for her merit before God is higher." Thus was Brigit saved from bondage.

Not long thereafter came a certain man of good kin unto Dubthach to ask for his daughter in marriage. Dubthach and his sons were willing, but Brigit refused. A brother of her brethren said to her: "Idle is the pure eye in thy head, not to be on a bolster beside a husband."

Said Brigit: "The Son of the Virgin knoweth, it is not lively for us if it bring harm upon us."

Then she put her finger under her eye and plucked it out of her head, so that it lay on her cheek. When Dubthach and her brethren beheld her, they promised that she should never be told to go to a husband save the husband whom she should like. Then Brigit put her palm to her eye, and it was healed at once.

Brigit and certain virgins along with her went to take the veil from Bishop Mel in Telcha Mide. Blithe was he to see them. For humility Brigit stayed so that she might be the last to whom a veil should be given. A fiery pillar rose from her head to the roof-ridge of the church. Then said Bishop Mel: "Come, O holy Brigit, that a veil may be sained on thy head before the other virgins."

It came to pass then, through the grace of the Holy Ghost, that the form of ordaining a Bishop was read over Brigit. Mac-caille said that a bishop's order should not be conferred on a woman.

Said Bishop Mel: "No power have I in this matter. That dignity hath been given by God unto Brigit, beyond every woman." Wherefore the men of Ireland from that time to this give episcopal honour to Brigit's successor.

After that Brigit founded a holy household with the other maidens. There came a time when they saw Patrick and his following coming to them. Said Lassair to Brigit, "What shall we do for the multitude that has come to us?"

"What food have ye?" asked Brigit.

"There is naught save one sheep and twelve loaves, and a little milk," said Lassair.

Said Brigit, "That is good: the preaching of God's word will be made unto us and we shall be satisfied thereby."

When Patrick had finished the preaching the food

was brought to Brigit that she might divide it. And she blessed it; and the two peoples of God, even Brigit's congregation and Patrick's congregation, were satisfied; and their leavings were much more than the material that had been there at first.

Brigit went to Bishop Mel that he might come and mark out her city for her. When they came thereafter to the place in which Kildare stands today, that was the time that Ailill, son of Dunlaing, chanced to be coming with a hundred horseloads of peeled rods, over the midst of Kildare. Then maidens came from Brigit to ask for some of the rods, and refusal was given to them. The horses were straightway struck down under their horseloads to the ground. Then stakes and wattles were taken from them, and they arose not until Ailill had offered the hundred horseloads to Brigit. And therewith was built Saint Brigit's great house in Kildare, and it is Ailill that fed the wrights and paid them their wages. So Brigit left a blessing that the kingship of Leinster should be till Doomsday from Ailill, son of Dunlaing.

Once upon a time Brigit beheld a certain man passing her with salt on his back.

"What is on thy back?" said Brigit.

"Stones," said the man.

"They shall be stones then," said Brigit. Straightway stones were made of the salt.

The same man came again past Brigit.

"What is on thy back?" said Brigit.

"Salt," said he.

"It shall be salt then," said Brigit.

Salt was at once made of the stones through Brigit's word.

Once seven bishops came and found Brigit in a place on the northern side of Kildare. Brigit asked her cook, even Blathnait, whether she had any food. She said she had none. Brigit was ashamed not to have food for the holy men, and she besought the Lord fervently. So the angels told her to milk the cows for the third time that day. Brigit herself milked the cows, and they filled the tubs with the milk, and they would have filled even all the vessels of Leinster. And the milk overflowed the vessels, and made a lake thereof, whence Loch in Ais, that is the "Lake of Milk" today. God's name and Brigit's were magnified thereby.

For everything that Brigit would ask of the Lord was granted her at once. For this was her desire: to satisfy the poor, to expel every hardship, to spare every miserable man. Now there never hath been anyone more bashful or more modest, or more gentle, or more humble, or more harmonious, or sager than Brigit. She never washed her hands or her feet or her head among men. She never looked at the face of a man. She never spoke without blushing. She was abstinent, she was innocent, she was prayerful, she was patient, she was glad in God's commandments: she was firm, she was humble, she was forgiving, she was loving: she was a consecrated casket for keeping Christ's Body and Blood: she was a temple of God. Her heart and her mind were a throne of rest for the Holy Ghost. She was simple towards God: she was compassionate towards the wretched: she was splendid in miracles and marvels: wherefore her name among created things is Dove among birds, Vine among trees, Sun among stars. This is the father of that holy virgin, the Heavenly Father: this is her son, Jesus Christ: this is her fosterer, the Holy Ghost: wherefore this holy virgin performs the great marvels and the innumerable miracles.

It is she that helpeth every one who is in a strait and

in danger: it is she that abateth the pestilences: it is she
that quelleth the anger and the storm of the sea. She is
the prophetess of Christ: she is the Queen of the South:
she is the Mary of the Gael.

Adapted from The Lives of the Saints
from 'The Book of Lismore'

Invocation to Bride

The genealogy of the holy maiden Bride,
Radiant flame of gold, noble foster-mother of
    Christ.
Bride the daughter of Dugall the brown,
Son of Aodh, son of Art, son of Conn,
Son of Crearar, son of Cis, son of Carmac, son of
    Carruin.

Every day and every night
That I say the genealogy of Bride,
I shall not be killed, I shall not be harried,
I shall not be put in cell, I shall not be wounded,
Neither shall Christ leave me in forgetfulness.

No fire, no sun, no moon shall burn me,
No lake, no water, nor sea shall drown me,
No arrow of fairy nor dart of fay shall wound me,
And I under the protection of my Holy Mary,
And my gentle foster-mother is my beloved Bride.

Carmina Gadelica

The Hermit's Song

I wish, O Son of the living God, O ancient, eternal
    King,
For a hidden little hut in the wilderness that it may
    be my dwelling.

An all-grey little lake to be by its side.
A clear pool to wash away sins through the grace
    of the Holy Spirit.

Quite near, a beautiful wood around it on every
    side,
To nurse many-voiced birds, hiding it with its
    shelter.

A southern aspect for warmth, a little brook across
    its floor,
A choice land with many gracious gifts such as be
    good for every plant.

A few men of sense — we will tell their number —
Humble and obedient, to pray to the King: —

Four times three, three times four, fit for every
    need,
Twice six in the church, both north and south: —

Six pairs beside myself,
Praying for ever the King who makes the sun shine.

A pleasant church with linen altar-cloth, a dwelling
    for God of Heaven;
Then, shining candles above the pure white
    Scriptures.

One house for all to go for the care of the body,
Without ribaldry, without boasting, without
    thought of evil.

This is the husbandry I would take, I would
    choose, and will not hide it:
Fragrant leek, hens, speckled salmon, trout, bees.

Raiment and food enough for me from the King
    of fair fame,
And I to be sitting for a while praying God in
    every place.

Translated by Kuno Meyer

Findian of Clonard, Tutor of Saints

In the time when Findian's mother was pregnant with him, there appeared to her a flame of fire which came into her mouth and went back by the same way in the form of a bright bird, and the bird went and sat on the branch of a tree. All the birds and birdflocks of Mogh's Half [the southern half of Ireland] came to it on that tree and stayed with it there. And the bird then went into Conn's Half [the northern half of Ireland], and sat there upon the branch of another tree. The birds and the birdflocks of Ireland came to it and it kept them with it.

When Findian grew up, he was taken to a bishop to Forthchernn, and read the Psalms and the ecclesiastical orders with him. Now, when he reached the age of thirty, he went over the sea to Gaul and was for thirty years studying in the monasteries there. One day the monks went into the wood to cut trees for the church. They did not ask Findian to go with them because of their honour for him. After they had gone came the sub-prior to Findian and asked why he had not gone into the wood.

"We should have gone long ago," said Findian, "had we been told to do so: now when it *is* said, we will go, provided the means are found by us."

"There are," said the sub-prior, "two young stags there in the field: yoke them and go into the wood."

Two angels of the God of Heaven met Findian and constrained the stags. Findian then took the stags into the wood, and his load was the first load that reached the church.

There came a desire to Findian to go to Rome after completing his studies. But God's angel came to him and said: "What would be given thee at Rome will be given thee here. Go and renew faith and belief in Ireland after Patrick." So Findian went to Ireland.

After a time Findian went over the Boyne to Clonard and founded a church in that place. Thereafter the saints of Ireland came to him from every point to learn wisdom by him, so that there were three thousand saints along with him; and of them, as the learned know, he chose the twelve high bishops of Ireland.* And the learned and the writings declare that no one of those three thousands went from him without a crozier, or a gospel, or some well-known sign; and round those reliquaries they built their churches and monasteries afterwards.

Once he sent his pupil, even Bishop Senach, to find out what the folk of his school were doing. Different, in sooth, was that at which each of them was found, yet all were good. Columb, son of Crimthann, was found with his hands stretched forth, and his mind contemplative in God, and birds resting on his hands and on his head. When that was told to Findian he said: "The hands of that man shall give me sacrifice and communion at the ending days."

Gemman the Master once took to Saint Findian an eulogy made in rhythm. "Neither gold, nor silver, nor precious raiment," said Gemman, "do I ask thee for

---

* Columba of Iona, Ciaran of Clonmacnoise, Brendan of Clonfert, Brendan of Birr, Molaisse of Devenish, Ciaran of Saighir, Canice of Aghaboe, Senell of Cluain Inis, Colman of Terryglass, Mobhi of Glasnevin, Nannidh of Inis Maige Samh, and Ruadham of Lothra. Thus Findian is known as the patriach of Irish monasticism.

this eulogy, but one thing only; the little land which I have is barren; wouldst thou make prayer that it become fruitful?"

Said Findian: "Put the hymn which thou hast made into water, and scatter that water over the land." This was done, and the land became fruitful.

From the Lives of the Saints from the "Book of Lismore"

Eltut of Llantwit

Llantwit was the school of the famous master of the Britons, Eltut by name. Now this Eltut was a disciple of Germanus, and Germanus himself had ordained him priest in his youth. And in truth Eltut was of all the Britons the most accomplished in all the Scriptures, namely of the Old and New Testaments, and in those of philosophy of every kind, of geometry namely, and of rhetoric, grammar and arithmetic, and of all the theories of philosophy. And by birth he was a wise magician, having knowledge of the future.

From the Life of St Samson of Dol

The Holy Man

He is a bird round which a trap is closed,
A leaking ship unfit for a wild sea,
An empty vessel and a withered tree,
Who lays aside God's wishes unimposed.
He is the sun's bright rays, pure gold and fine,
A silver chalice overfilled with wine,
Holy and happy, beautiful in love —
Who does the will of God in Heav'n above.

Translated by Molloy Carson

Senan of Inis Cathaig

There came a year of drought to Inis Cathaig where Senan had set up a monastery. His household came to lament to him that they had no water. Then an angel of God came to converse with Senan after nocturns, and said: "Greatly do thy household complain that they are without water; go that we may see the place wherein there is water nearby."

Senan and the angel arose at once and went to the spot where the water is today. The angel said, "Dig thou here."

Senan took a stick of holly and dug as the angel had said. As Senan dug, the angel cleansed. Then the angel said: "Sufficient is its depth which thou diggest; there will be no want of water in this well so long as there shall be habitation in this church, and it will heal every illness which shall be brought to it."

Then Senan set the holly stick on the brink of the well, and it took the soil at once. On the morrow, as the brethren arose, they beheld the well full of water and a full-grown tree of holly on its brink. . .

Now Brigit, daughter of Cu Cathrach, a virginal holy maiden, had set up a church on Cluain Infide, on the brink of the Shannon. She had a chasuble as alms for Senan, and she had no messenger, so she made a little basket of rods of holly, and she put moss to it, and placed the chasuble in it along with a sign to Senan asking for the sacrifice. Then she set the basket upon the Shannon, and said to the river: "Thou hast leave to bear that with thee to Inis Cathaig."

On the day that the chasuble came to Inis Cathaig, Senan said to his deacon, "If thou findest aught on the strand, thou hast leave to bring it hither."

The deacon found the basket and carried it to Senan, who put on the chasuble. Therefore two stones of salt were put into the same basket, and the box containing the Sacrifice was also put in, and the basket was set upon the same water.

Senan said to the river: "Thou hast leave to carry this to Cluain Infide and display the box and the one piece of salt to Brigit, and thou take the other piece of salt to Inis Clothrann to Diarmait."

When the basket reached Cluain Infide, Brigit went to it and took out the box and one of the two pieces of salt. The stream of the Shannon then swept away the basket and left it in Inis Clothrann with Diarmait . . .

Canair the Pious, a holy maiden of the Benntraige of the south of Ireland, set up a hermitage in her own territory. There one night after nocturns, she was praying, when all the churches of Ireland appeared to her. And it seemed that a tower of fire rose up to heaven from each of the churches; but the greatest of the towers, and the straightest towards heaven, was that which rose from Inis Cathaig. "Fair is yon cell," said she. "Thither will I go, that my resurrection may be near it." Straightway on she went, without guidance save the tower of fire which she beheld ablaze without ceasing day and night before her, till she came thither. Now, when she had reached the shore of Luimnech, she crossed the sea with dry feet as if she were on smooth land, till she came to Inis Cathaig. Now Senan knew that thing, and he went to the harbour to meet her, and he gave her welcome.

"Yea, I have come," said Canair.

"Go," said Senan, "to thy sister who dwells in yon

77

island in the east, that thou mayest have guesting therein."

"Not for that have we come," said Canair, "but that I may have guesting with *thee* in *this* island."

"Women enter not this island," said Senan.

"How canst thou say that?" said Canair. "Christ is no worse than thou. Christ came to redeem women no less than to redeem men. No less did He suffer for the sake of women than for the sake of men. Women have given service and tendance unto Christ and His Apostles. No less than men do women enter the heavenly kingdom. Why, then, shouldst thou not take women to thee in thine island?"

"Thou art stubborn," said Senan.

"What then," said Canair, "shall I get what I ask for, a place for my side in this isle and the Sacrament from thee to me?"

"A place of resurrection," said Senan, "will be given thee here on the brink of the wave, but I fear the sea will carry off thy remains."

"God will grant me," said Canair, "that the spot wherein I shall lie will not be the first that the sea will bear away."

"Thou hast leave then," said Senan, "to come on shore." For thus had she been while they were in conversation, standing up on the wave, with her staff under her bosom, as if she were on land. Then Canair came on shore, and the Sacrament was administered to her, and she straightway went to heaven.

God granted unto Canair that whoso visits her church before going on the sea shall not be drowned between going and returning.

From the Lives of the Saints from the "Book of Lismore"

78

The Sea

Look you out
northeastwards
over mighty ocean,
    teeming with sea-life;
home of seals,
sporting, splendid,
its tide has reached
    fullness.

Translated by James Carney

Brendan of Clonfert, the Navigator

Now, on the night of Brendan's birth, bishop Eirc, of Alltraige, beheld a wood under one vast flame, the like whereof had never before been seen by him, and the manifold service of the angels in bright-white garments all around the land. At the end of a year Eirc took the child with him to his own foster-mother, even Ita, and Brendan remained five years with her. And the nun gave him exceeding love, for she used to see the service of angels above him, and the grace of the Holy Spirit manifested upon him; and it is thus that Brendan used to be, calling continually to the nun whenever he would see her. Now on a certain day Ita said to him: "What is it that causes thee joy, my holy child?"

"Thou," said he, "whom I see speaking to me continually, and many other innumerable virgins like thee, and they together fostering me from one hand to another." Now those were angels in the forms of the virgins.

Angels in the forms of white virgins
Were fostering Brendan
From one hand to another,
Without much disgrace to the babe.

Then Brendan studied, and learnt the canon of the Old Law and the New Testament, after which he desired to write and to learn the Rules of the Saints of Ireland. Now after he had written these Rules of the Saints, with their usages and with their piety, he returned to bishop Eirc and received ecclesiastical orders from him. There he heard in the Gospel: "Every one that hath forsaken father or mother or sister or lands for my name's sake shall receive a hundredfold in the present, and shall possess everlasting life." After that, then, the love of God grew exceedingly in his heart, and he desired to leave his land and his country, his parents and his fatherland.

So Brendan, son of Finnlug, sailed then with some chosen men over the wave-voice of the strong-maned sea, and over the storm of the green-sided waves, and over the mouths of the marvellous, awful, bitter ocean, where they saw the multitude of the furious red-mouthed monsters, with abundance of the great sea-whales. And they found beautiful marvellous islands, and yet they tarried not therein.

Thus they abode for the space of five years on the ocean marvellous, strange, unknown to them. And during that time not one of them departed, and they suffered loss of none of their people, and body or soul of not one of them was injured. And that was a marvel, for Brendan had not let them take provisions with them; but he said that God was able to feed them wheresoever they might be, even as He fed the five thousand with the five loaves and the two fishes.

One time they found a maiden, smooth, full-grown, yellow-haired, whiter than snow or the foam of the wave; and she was dead, the blow of a spear having gone through her shoulder and passed between her two paps. Huge in sooth was the size of that maiden, to wit, a hundred feet in her height, and nine feet between her two paps, and seven feet in the length of her middle finger. Brendan brought her to life at once, and then he baptized her and asked her concerning her kindred. "Of the inhabitants of the sea am I," said she, "that is, of those who pray and expect their resurrection."

Now when the Easter was nigh, his family kept saying to Brendan that he should go on land to celebrate the Easter. "God," said Brendan, "is able to give us land in any place that He pleases." Now after Easter had come, the great sea-beast raised his shoulder on high over the storm and over the wave-voice of the sea, so that it was level, firm land, like a field equally smooth, equally high. And they go forth upon that land and there they celebrate the Easter, even one day and two nights. After they had gone on board their vessels, the whole plunged straightway under the sea. And it was in that wise they used to celebrate the Easter, to the end of seven years, on the back of the whale.

Brendan loved lasting devotion
According to synod and company:
Seven years on the back of the whale:
Hard was the rule of devotion.

For when the Easter of every year was at hand, the whale would heave up his back, so that it was dry and solid land.

From the Lives of the Saints from the "Book of Lismore"

The Three

The Three Who are over me,
The Three Who are below me,
The Three Who are above me here,
The Three Who are above me yonder,
The Three Who are in the earth,
The Three Who are in the air,
The Three Who are in the heaven,
 The Three who are in the great pouring sea.

Carmina Gadelica

The World

Take no oath, take no oath
    by the sod you stand upon:
you walk it short while
    but your burial is long.

Pay no heed, pay no heed
    to the world and its way,
give no love, give no love
    to what lasts but a day.

Have no care, have no care
    for the meaningless earth.
lay no hold, lay no hold
    on its gaiety and mirth.

A man fair of face
    was here yesterday;
now he is nothing
    but blood beneath clay.

The world is running out
    like the ebbing sea:
fly far from it
    and seek safety.

Translated by James Carney

Kevin of Glendalough

An angel appeared to Kevin and commanded him to enter an order of monks for instruction, and he submitted to ordination and became an elect priest. The angel afterwards told him to go into the desert glen which had been foretold to him, that is, to the slope of the lakes of Glendalough. Great was Kevin's courage in separating from the glory and beauty of the present life, and remaining in solitude listening to the converse of the angel who ministered to him. He would lie by night on bare stones on the border of the lake; skins of wild beasts were his clothing. He would cross the lake without any boat to the rock to say Mass every day, and remained without fear or dread above the lake. Seven years was he without food but nettles and sorrel; and for a long period of years he never saw a human being; and he would stand up to his waist in the lake saying his hours.

One time when Kevin was reciting his hours, he dropped his psalter into the lake; and great grief and vexation seized him. Afterwards an otter came to him, bringing the psalter from the bottom of the lake, and not a line or letter was blotted.

Kevin was accustomed all his life through the severity of his asceticism to spend every Lent in a wattled pen, with a gray flagstone under him as a bed, and his only food the music of the angels; and he would spend a fortnight and a month thus. And one Lent when he was acting in this way, a blackbird came from the wood to his pen, and hopped on his palm as he lay on the flagstone with his hand stretched out; and he kept his hand in that position so that the blackbird built its nest in it, and hatched her brood. The angel came to Kevin and bade him leave the penance, but Kevin said that the pain of his hand being under the blackbird till she hatched her brood was little compared with the pain which his Lord suffered for his sake.

It occurred to the king of Leinster to send a son who had been born to him to Kevin to be baptized. And he sent word that Kevin should keep the boy under his protection, because every son that had been previously born to him had been destroyed by the bright people of fairy courts. And when the infant came to Kevin to be baptized, a fairy witch named Cainleog, with her attendant women, followed the infant, bent on destroying him, as they had destroyed the other sons of the king. When Kevin noticed this, he cursed the women, and thereupon they were turned into stones, and they remain thenceforth in the form of stones on the brink of the lake which is in the glen. And Kevin loved the infant, and took him as his foster-child.

Now there were neither cows nor boolies in the glen at that time, so it was a great problem for Kevin how he should find sustenance and milk to nourish the infant; and this caused him anxiety. However, as he looked behind him he saw a doe in milk, and a little fawn following her; and when Kevin saw this, he prayed God earnestly to tame the doe, so that it might come and yield its milk to the infant. And thereupon the doe came gently to Kevin and forthwith dropped milk onto a hollow stone both for the infant and for her own fawn. So that this is the definite name of the place where the stone is, Innis Eilte (the doe's milking stead) thenceforward. In this way the doe came every day to drop her milk on the hollow stone, so that sufficient for the infant's nourishment was obtained.

However, one day when the doe went to graze in the wood, a wolf came out of a hollow of the rock and killed the fawn and devoured it. When Kevin saw this, he ordered the wolf to go gently to the doe in place of the fawn; and the wolf did so habitually. Thereupon the doe would drop her milk on the stone to feed the infant as she formerly did for her fawn, though there was only a wolf standing at her breast. Thus the child was nurtured, and became a disciple of Kevin.

. . . Afterwards, a great number of pilgrims out of every quarter of Ireland came to visit Kevin's church; so that this is one of the four chief pilgrimages of Erin: to wit, the Cave of Patrick in Ulster, Croagh Patrick in Connaught, the Isle of the Living in Munster, and Glendalough in Leinster.

From the Lives of Irish Saints

Oratory, Gallarus

*Figures on the Shrine
of St Mogue (Maedoc)*

Maedoc and Molaisse

One day Maedoc and another disciple named Molaisse
were praying at the foot of two trees, and they loved
each other very dearly. "Ah! Jesus," said they, "is it
Thy will that we should part, or that we should remain
together to the end?"

Then one of the two trees fell to the south, and the
other to the north. "By the fall of the trees," said they,
"it has been revealed that we must part."

Maedoc fared south, and built a noble monastery at
Ferns, and Molaisse fared north, and built a monastery
in Devenish.

From the Lives of Irish Saints

Mo Chua's Riches

Mo Chua and Colum Cille were contemporaries. And when he was in a hermitage in the wilderness, Mo Chua had no worldly wealth but a cock and a mouse and a fly. The work the cock used to do for him was to keep matins at midnight. Now, the mouse would not allow him to sleep more than five hours in a day and a night; and when he wished to sleep longer, being tired from much cross-vigil and prostration, the mouse would begin nibbling his ear, and so awoke him. Then the fly, the work it did was to walk along every line he read in his psalter, and when he rested from singing his psalms the fly would stay on the line he had left until he returned again to read his psalms. It happened that after a time these three treasures died; and Mo Chua wrote a letter afterwards to Colum Cille when he was in Iona in Scotland, and complained of the death of this flock. Colum Cille wrote to him, and this is what he said: "Brother," said he, "you must not wonder at the death of the flock that has gone from you, for misfortune never comes but where there are riches."

From Keating's History of Ireland

Pangur Ban

I and Pangur Ban my cat,
'Tis a like task we are at:
Hunting mice is his delight,
Hunting words I sit all night.

Better far than praise of men
'Tis to sit with book and pen;
Pangur bears me no ill will,
He too plies his simple skill.

'Tis a merry thing to see
At our tasks how glad are we,
When at home we sit and find
Entertainment to our mind.

Oftentimes a mouse will stray
In the hero Pangur's way;
Oftentimes my keen thought set
Takes a meaning in its net.

'Gainst the wall he set his eye
Full and fierce and sharp and sly;
'Gainst the wall of knowledge I
All my little wisdom try.

When a mouse darts from its den
O how glad is Pangur then!
O what gladness do I prove
When I solve the doubts I love!

So in peace our tasks we ply,
Pangur Ban, my cat, and I;
In our arts we find our bliss,
I have mine and he has his.

Practice every day has made
Pangur perfect in his trade;
I get wisdom day and night
Turning darkness into light.

Translated by Robin Flower

Straying Thoughts

My thought it is a wanton ranger,
It skips away;
I fear 'twill bring my soul in danger
On Judgment Day.

For when the holy psalms are singing
Away it flies,
Gambolling, stumbling, lightly springing
Before God's eyes.

'Mongst giddypated folk it rambles,
Girls light of mind;
Through forests and through cities gambols
Swifter than wind.

Now in rich raths with jewels glowing
'Mid goodly men;
Now to the ragged pauper going
'Tis fled again.

Without a boat it skims the ocean,
'Tis swift to fly
Heavenward with unimpeded motion
From earth to sky.

Through all the courses of all folly
It runs, and then
Lightly, untouched of melancholy
Comes home again.

Vain is the hope to hold or bind it,
The unfettered thought
Wanton, unresting, idle-minded,
Sets chains at nought.

The sword's keen edge, the whip's sharp chiding
It scorns, grown bold;
Like an eel's tail it wriggles, sliding
Out of my hold.

No bolt, no bar, no lock, no fetter,
No prison cell
Can stay its course; they serve no better,
Pits deep as Hell.

O fair, chaste Christ! who in all places
Seest all men's eyes
Check by the Spirit's sevenfold graces
Thought's wandering wise.

Terrible Lord of earth and heaven!
Rule Thou my heart!
My faith, my love to Thee be given,
My every part!

So in thy companies to-morrow
I too may go;
Loyal and leal are they. My sorrow!
I am not so.

Translated by Robin Flower

Ciaran of Clonmacnoise

One day when Ciaran was but a young boy his mother blamed him, saying, "The other little lads of the hamlet bring honey out of the honeycombs home to their households, and thou bringest none to us." When Ciaran heard that, he went to a certain well, and filled his vessel out of it, and blessed it, so that it became choice honey, and gave that honey to his mother, and she was thankful. And that is the honey which was given to deacon Justus as his fee for baptizing Ciaran.

Now this was the work that his parents gave him to do, even herding cattle after the manner of David, son of Jesse, and of Jacob. For God knew that he would be a prudent herdsman to great herds, that is, the herds of the faithful. After that there came to pass something marvellous at Rath Cremthainn while he was herding the cattle of his foster-father, deacon Justus at Fidarta, there being a long distance between them. Howbeit, Ciaran used to hear what his tutor had to say as if they had been side by side. Then came a fox to Ciaran out of the wood, and Ciaran dealt gently with it; and it used to visit him often, until at last he enjoined upon it to do him a service, namely to carry his psalter between him and his tutor, deacon Justus. For when it was said at Fidarta, "Say this in the name of the Father, and of the Son, and of the Holy Ghost," Ciaran at Rath Cremthainn used to hear from that to the end of the lesson. And the fox used to be humbly attending the lesson till the writing of it on wax came to an end, and he then would take it with him to Ciaran. But once his natural malice broke through the fox, and he began to eat the book, for he was greedy about the leathern bands that were about it on the outside. While he was eating the book, then came Oengus, son of Crimthann, with a band of men and with greyhounds. And they hunted the fox, and he found no shelter in any place till he came under Ciaran's cowl. God's name and Ciaran's were magnified by saving the book from the fox, and by saving the fox from the hounds.

On a certain day Ciaran's mother was making blue dye-stuff, and she was ready to put the cloth in it. She then asked Ciaran to go out of the house, for they did not deem it right or lucky to have men in the same house in which cloth was being dyed.

"Let there be a dark-grey stripe in it then." said Ciaran.

So of all the cloth that was put into the dye-stuff, there was none without a dark-grey stripe therein. The dye-stuff was again prepared, and his mother said to him, "Go out now this time, Ciaran; and, O Ciaran, let there not be now a dark-grey stripe therein!"

Then Ciaran said: "May my foster-mother's dye-stuff be white! Let it be whiter than bone! Every time it shall come out of the boiling let it be whiter than curd!"

And every cloth that was put into it became all white.

The dye-stuff was prepared the third time. "O Ciaran," said his mother, "do not now spoil the dye-stuff for me; but let it be blessed by thee."

So when Ciaran blessed it there never was made, before or after, dye-stuff as good as it; for though all the cloth of the neighbours were put into it, it made all blue, and finally the residue made blue the dogs and cats that touched it and the trees against which they came.

Once Ciaran was herding kine. A most wretched wolf came to him, and Ciaran said: "May mercy come to us! Go and eat the calf, and break not and eat not its bones." The wolf went and did so.

When the cow lowed a-seeking the calf, Ciaran's mother said to him: "Tell me, Ciaran, in what place is this cow's calf? Let the calf come from thee, whatsoever death it suffered."

Ciaran went to the spot in which the wolf had devoured the calf, and he gathered the calf's bones, and put them in front of the cow, and the calf arose and stood up.

After these things it was time for Ciaran to go as a scholar to Findian of Clonard in order to learn wisdom. So he asked his mother and father for a cow, that he might take her with him when he went to learn. His mother said she would not give him a cow, so he blessed a cow of the kine — *Odar Ciarain* ("Ciaran's Dun") was her name thenceforward — and she went thence with her calf after Ciaran to Clonard. And there was no fence between them, so Ciaran drew between them a line with his staff, and the cow was licking the calf, and neither of them would come over that mark. Now the milk of that cow was parted among those twelve bishops with their households and their guests, and it used to be enough for them all.

Once upon a time the king of Cualann's daughter was brought to Findian to read her psalms, after having dedicated her maidenhood to God. Findian entrusted the girl to Ciaran, and with him she used to read her psalms. Now, so long as they remained together, Ciaran saw nothing of the girl's body save only her feet.

Then twelve lepers came to Findian to be healed. Findian sent them on to Ciaran. Ciaran made them

94

welcome, and went with them westward from the church, and cut a sod out of the earth, whereupon a stream of pure water broke forth. He poured three waves of that water over each of the men, and they were at once every whit whole.

In this school, moreover, a stag used to visit Ciaran, and he used to put his book on the deer's horns. One day there Ciaran heard the bell. He rose up suddenly at the bell; howbeit the stag arose more swiftly, and went forth with the book on his horns. Though that day was wet and the night after it, and though the book was open, not a single letter in it was moistened. On the morrow the cleric arose, and the deer came to him with the book all safe.

Now when it was time for Ciaran to go from Clonard after learning reading and wisdom, he left the Dun with holy Ninnidh, but he said that her hide would come to him afterwards. And Ciaran said besides that though a multitude would be helped by her milk, there would be more to whom her hide would give help, for what soul soever separated from its body on that hide inhabits eternal life.*

Findian beheld a vision of Ciaran and Columba, even two moons in the air, with a hue of gold upon them. One of the two went by sea to the northeast; the other went to the Shannon and shone over the middle of Ireland. Those were Columba in Iona with the radiance of his nobleness and his high birth, and Ciaran at Clonmacnoise with the radiance of his charity and his mercy.

Then Ciaran went his way, with Findian's blessing, after which Columba bore this witness upon him:

---

*Legend has it that the hide of Ciaran's Dun became the parchment used for the *Lebar na h'Uidre* (*Book of the Dun Cow*), a twelth-century collection of ancient Irish history, genealogy, and literature compiled by a Clonmacnoise scribe.

A marvellous hero goes from us westward,
Ciaran, son of the wright,
Without greed, without pride, without reviling,
Without lust, without satire.

Thereafter Ciaran went to Aran to commune with Enna. And the two, even Ciaran and Enna, beheld the same vision, to wit, a great fruitful tree beside a stream in the middle of Ireland; and it protected the island of Ireland, and its fruit went forth over the sea that surrounds the island, and the birds of the world came to carry off somewhat of its fruit. Ciaran related the vision to Enna. Said Enna: "The great tree which thou beheldst is thou thyself, for thou art great in the eyes of God and men, and all of Ireland will be full of thy honour. This island will be protected under the shadow of thy favour, and multitudes will be satisfied with the grace of thy fasting and thy prayer. Go then with God's word to a bank of a stream, and there found a church."

When Ciaran went out of Aran, a poor man met him on the path. Ciaran gave his linen chasuble to him, and then went to Inis Cathaig to bid farewell to Senan. Since he had nothing on but his one mantle, that was revealed to Senan; and Senan went to meet him with a robe under his armpit. Afterwards, when Ciaran had come to Clonmacnoise, he desired to send another robe to Senan. This robe was placed in the stream of the Shannon, and it went on down the stream without getting wet to the harbour of Inis Cathaig.

Senan said to his monks, "Go to the sea, and ye will find a guest there, and bring it with you, with honour and veneration."

When the monks went out, they found the robe on the sea, and it was dry, and they brought it to Senan, and he gave thanks to God.

After Ciaran left Senan he went to his brethren to

Isel, and there he dwelt for a time. And one day he was doing his lesson out on the field, when he went to visit his guests, and left the book open till morning, under the wet. And not a damp drop came to the book.

Now when the brethren were unable to endure Ciaran's charity because of its greatness, and when envy seized them, they sent him away. Then Ciaran put his books on the back of a stag, and the stag used to accompany him on every path by which he would go. The stag went before him to Inis Angin, so Ciaran entered that island and dwelt there.

It happened that Ciaran's gospel was dropped into the lake by a certain careless brother, and it remained for a long while under the lake. On a certain day in summer-time cows went into the lake, and the strap of the gospel stuck to the foot of one of the cows, and from below she brought with her the Gospel to land. Now when it was opened, thus it was: white, dry, without loss of a letter, all through Ciaran's grace.

Three years and three months dwelt Ciaran in Inis Angin, and after that he came to Clonmacnoise on the Shannon. Said Ciaran to his eight companions: "Here we will stay, for many souls will go to heaven hence, and there will be a visit from God and from men for ever on this place." Marvellous, then, was that monastery which was set up by Ciaran with his eight.

Howbeit, Ciaran remained in that place for the space of seven months only, when he went to heaven on the ninth day of the middle month of autumn. When the time of his decease drew nigh to the holy Ciaran in the thirty-third year of his age, he was carried into the little church, and he raised his hands and blessed his people, and told the brethren to shut him up in the church until Kevin should come from Glendalough. When after three days Kevin arrived, he did not at once receive the

97

full courtesy of the clerics, for they were in grief and great sorrow after their cleric.

Said Kevin to them, "A look of moroseness be on you always."

Then great fear seized the elders, and they did Kevin's will, and opened the little church before him. Ciaran's spirit at once went to heaven, and came again into its body to commune with Kevin, and made welcome to him; and they were there from the one watch to another, in mutual conversation, and making their union. Then Ciaran blessed Kevin, and Kevin blessed water and administered communion to Ciaran. And then Ciaran gave his bell to Kevin in sign of their unity.

Now the saints of Ireland envied Ciaran for his goodness, and they betook themselves to the King of Heaven that his life might be shortened. So great was the envy which they had for him that even his own comrade, Columba, said: "Blessing on God who took this holy Ciaran! For if he had remained until he was an ancient man, he would not have found the place of two chariot-horses in Ireland that would not have been his."

From the Lives of the Saints from the "Book of Lismore"

Jesu who Ought to be Praised

It were as easy for Jesu
To renew the withered tree
As to wither the new
Were it His will so to do.
   Jesu! Jesu! Jesu!
   Jesu who ought to be praised.

There is no life in the sea,
There is no creature in the river,
There is naught in the firmament,
But proclaims His goodness.
   Jesu! Jesu! Jesu!
   Jesu who ought to be praised.

There is no bird on the wing,
There is no star in the sky,
There is nothing beneath the sun,
But proclaims His goodness.
   Jesu! Jesu! Jesu!
   Jesu who ought to be praised.

Carmina Gadelica

Mochuda of Rahen and Lismore

Once as Mochuda was praying by himself he saw a man named Magus coming to him, who said to him mockingly, "Bring leaves on to that apple tree by thee."

Mochuda made the sign of the Cross over the apple tree, and it was all covered with leaves.

"It were more beautiful with blossom on it," said Magus.

Mochuda produced the blossom as was said to him.

"It were better if there were apples on it," said Magus.

Mochuda did this, and it was fully laden with apples.

"It were better that they were ripe," said Magus, "so that we may eat them."

This was fulfilled so that they came down in a ripe shower on the ground by the apple tree.

Magus took up an apple to eat it, for they seemed to him desirable for their size and beauty; but he could not eat it by reason of its sourness.

"It were better not to produce them," said Magus, "than to produce them with such sourness."

Mochuda blessed them then, and they had the taste of honey.

Thereupon Magus departed, and he was blinded at Mochuda's word for a year because of the incredulity which he had shown. At the end of the year he submitted to Mochuda's judgment, and was healed of his blindness after penance, and was a monk of Mochuda's as long as he lived.

Another Story about Mochuda

Mochuda of Rahen was carving one evening for his convent and for his guests there. Now whenever his hands happened to touch any of the food, he would rub his hands on his shoes which he wore daily. And one night Mochuda said: "Great is this authority in which I am; seven and seven score and seven hundred in this convent, and every third man of them has converse with angels, and I am abbot and head over them all, and yet I am the worst of them all. And this is no road to heaven for me, and I will not remain like this any longer, but will seek a ship that is leaving Ireland, and will not be two nights in one place, but I will be in penance throughout the length of the great world."

In this wise he spent the night, and the next day he escaped to the place where Comgall was, Tehelly. When they saw one another, they blessed one another.

"Sit down," said Comgall.

"I would rather not," said Mochuda, "for I am in a hurry; there is a ship about to sail, and I must go in her."

"Not so," said Comgall, "for God will cause the ship to remain here tonight."

So Mochuda sat down, and his shoes were taken off him, and as they were taken off Comgall said, "Come out, O devil, from the shoe; thou shalt not carry off any more the spoils which thou didst find."

At hearing this the devil leaped out of the shoe, and as he departed he said: "It was lucky for thee, thy falling in with Comgall, O Mochuda, for I would not have allowed thee to be two nights in the same place because of the unfair advantage which thou gavest to thine own shoes over the shoes of the convent, for thou wouldst rub thy hands on them when thou wert carving the monks' refection, and I found no other way of getting at thee but only this."

The devil thereupon departed, and Comgall said to the saint that he should return home, and attend to his hours. And he said:

It is good for a clerk to reside in one place
And attend the hours.
It is mocking devils that put
The spirit of restlessness in a man.

So Mochuda continued to reside without wandering, through the power of God and of Comgall.

From the Lives of Irish Saints

Columba's Farewell to Ireland

Delightful to be on the hill of Howth
Before going over the white-haired sea:
The dashing of the waves against its face,
The bareness of its shores and of its border.

Delightful to be on the hill of Howth
After coming over the white-bosomed sea;
To be rowing one's little coracle,
Alas! on the wild-waved shore.

Great is the speed of my coracle,
And its stern turned upon Derry:
Grievous is my errand over the main,
Travelling to Alba of the beetling brows.

My foot in my tuneful coracle,
My sad heart tearful:
A man without guidance is weak,
Blind are all the ignorant.

There is a grey eye
That will not look back upon Ireland:
It shall never see again
The men of Ireland nor her women.

Translated by Kuno Meyer

The Mysterious Sacrifice and Reward of Odran

When Columb Cille reached the place that today is called "Hi of Columb Cille" [Iona], he said to his household: "It is well for us that our roots should go underground here." And he said: "It is permitted to you that some one of you should go under the earth here or under the mould of the island to consecrate it." Odran rose up readily, and this he said: "If I should be taken," saith he, "I am ready for that." Saith Columb Cille: "O Odran! Thou shalt have the reward thereof. No prayer shall be granted to anyone at my grave unless it is first asked of thee." Then Odran went to heaven. Columb founded a church by him after that.

From the Lives of the Saints from the "Book of Lismore"

Behold Iona!
A blessing on each eye that seeth it!
He who does a good for others
Here, will find his own redoubled
Many-fold!

Attributed to Columba

A Conference with Angels*

The blessed man one day, while living in the Iouan island [Iona], the brethren being gathered together, charged them with great earnestness, saying, "Today I desire to go out alone into the western plain of our island; therefore let none of you follow me." And on their professing obedience, he goes out alone, as he wished. But a certain brother, a crafty, prying fellow, slipping off another way, secretly ensconces himself in the top of a certain little hill, which overlooks the same plain; desiring, you see, to find out the cause of that solitary expedition of the blessed man. And when the same spy, from the top of the hillock, beheld him standing on a certain little hill on that plain, praying with his hands spread out to heaven and lifting his eyes up to heaven, wonderful to say, behold! suddenly a marvellous sight appeared. For holy angels, citizens of the celestial country, flying to him with wonderful swiftness, and clothed in white robes, began to stand around the holy man as he prayed; and after some conversation with the blessed man, that heavenly host, as if perceiving itself to be under observation, quickly sped back to the highest heavens. And the blessed man himself, after the angelic conference, on his return to the monastery, again gathers the brethren together, and with no ordinary chiding inquires which of them is guilty of transgression. And, when they then declare that they do not know, the offender, conscious of his

*Unless otherwise noted the stories of Columba are taken from Adamnan's *Life of Columba*, written about one hundred years after Columba's death.

inexcusable transgression, and not enduring further to conceal his fault, on bended knees, in the midst of the choir of the brethren, as a suppliant, begs pardon before the Saint. The Saint, leading him aside, charges him with severe threatening, as he kneels before him, that to no man must he disclose anything, not even a little secret, concerning that angelic vision, during the life of the same blessed man. But after the departure of the holy man from the body, he related that apparition of the heavenly host to the brethren.

Columba and the Crane

At another time, when the Saint was living in the Iouan isle, he calls one of the brethren to him, and thus addresses him: "On the third day from this that is breaking, thou oughtest to sit on the sea-shore, and look out in the western part of this island; for from the northern part of Ireland a certain guest, a crane to wit, beaten by the winds during long and circuitous aerial flights, will arrive after the ninth hour of the day, very weary and fatigued, and, its strength being almost gone, it will fall down before thee and lie on the beach. Thou wilt take care to lift it up tenderly, and carry it to some neighbouring house; and while it is there hospitably received, thou wilt diligently feed it, attending to it for three days and three nights; and then, refreshed after the three days are fulfilled, and unwilling to sojourn any longer with us, it will return with fully recovered strength to its former sweet home in Scotia [Ireland] whence it came; and I so earnestly commend it to thee, because it comes from our fatherland."

The brother obeys, and on the third day, after the

ninth hour, as he had been bidden, he awaits the coming of the anticipated guest, and then, when it is come; fallen, he lifts it from the beach; weak, he bears it to the hospice; hungry, he feeds it. And when he has returned to the monastery in the evening, the Saint, not questioning, but declaring, says, "God bless thee, my son, for that thou hast well attended to our stranger guest, which will not tarry long in its wanderings, but after three days will return to its native land." Which the event also proved, just as the Saint predicted. For after being lodged for three days, it first lifted itself up on high by flying from the earth in the presence of its ministering host; then after looking out its way in the air for a little while, it crossed the ocean wave, and returned to Ireland in a straight course of flight on a calm day.

The Voice of St Columba

But we ought not to be silent respecting this tradition concerning the voice of the blessed man in chanting the Psalms, which has undoubtedly been handed down from some who put it to the test. Which voice of the venerable man chanting in the church with the brethren, lifted up in a wonderful manner, was sometimes heard for four furlongs, that is, five hundred paces, but sometimes even for eight furlongs, that is, a thousand paces. Wonderful to relate! In the ears of those who were standing with him in the church, his voice did not exceed the ordinary measure of the human voice in loudness of tone. But yet at the same hour those who were standing more than a thousand paces off heard the same voice so distinctly that they could even distinguish by the separate syllables what verses he was singing, for his voice sounded alike in the ears of those close at hand and of those who were listening at a distance. However, this miracle of the voice of the blessed man is not proved to have always occurred, but only on rare occasion, yet it could not have happened at all without the grace of the Divine Spirit.

But we must not be silent concerning what is said once to have taken place, in connection with such wonderful elevation of his voice, close to the fortress of King Brude. For while the Saint himself, with a few brethren, was conducting after their manner the evening praises of God outside the king's fortress, some Druids, coming nearer to them, tried to hinder them as much as possible, that the voice of Divine praise proceeding from their mouths might not be heard among the heathen people. As soon as he found this out, the Saint began to sing the forty-fourth psalm, and in a wonderful manner his voice was at that moment so lifted up in the air, like some dreadful thunder, that both king and people were affrighted by terror too great to be endured.

Columba and the Druid

After the above mentioned events had taken place, Broichan, the king's Druid, one day addresses himself to the holy man and says, "Tell me, Columba, what time dost thou propose to sail out?"

"On the third day," says the Saint, "if God will and I live, we propose to begin our voyage."

Broichan says in reply, "Thou wilt not be able, for

I can make the wind contrary for thee, and bring over thee a thick darkness."

The Saint says, "The Almighty power of God ruleth over all things, and in His Name all our movements are directed, Himself being our governor."

What more need be said? As he had proposed in his heart, so the Saint came on the aforesaid day to the long lake of the river Ness, accompanied by a great following. But the Druids then began to rejoice when they saw a thick darkness come over, with a contrary wind and tempest. It is no marvel that these things can sometimes be done by the artifice of demons, that even the winds and the seas are so stirred up into a more stormy condition.

Our Columba therefore, seeing the raging elements stirred against him, calls on Christ the Lord, and mounts the boat while the sailors are hesitating; he himself, with greater firmness, directs that the sail be hoisted up against the wind. Which being done, the whole multitude looking on, the craft flies along with amazing velocity, borne against adverse winds. And after no great space of time the contrary winds shift round to the help of the journey, and to the wonder of all. And so through all that day the boat of the blessed man was borne along by gentle and favourable breezes blowing, and landed at the desired haven. Let the reader therefore ponder well how great that venerable man was, and what manner of man, in whom Almighty God manifested His glorious Name in the sight of the heathen, by such miraculous powers as those above recorded.

The Song of Trust

I adore not the voice of birds,
Nor sneezing, nor lots in this world,
Nor a boy, nor lots, nor women:
My Druid is Christ, the son of God,
Christ, Son of Mary, the Great Abbot,
The Father, the Son, and the Holy Ghost.

Attributed to Columba

An Angel Saves a Brother

Once as the holy man was sitting writing in his little cell, suddenly his countenance is changed, and he pours forth this cry from his pure breast, saying, "Help! Help!"

Two brethren standing at the door, namely Colgu son of Cellach, and Lugne Mocublai, ask him the reason of such a sudden cry. To whom the venerable man gives this answer, saying, "I have directed the angel of the Lord, who was just now standing among you, with all haste to help one of the brethren who has fallen from the top of the roof of the great house which is at the present time being built in the Plain of the Oakwood [Durrow]."

And then the Saint added these words, saying, "How wonderful and almost unspeakable is the swiftness of angelic flight, equal, as I think, to the rapidity of lightning. For that heavenly spirit who just now flew away from us hence, when that man began to slip, came to his help as it were in the twinkling of an eye, and bore him up before he could touch the ground; nor could he who fell perceive any fracture or injury. How amazing, I say, is this most rapid and seasonable help, which, quicker than can be said, with such spaces of sea and land lying between, can so rapidly be rendered."

The Barley Field

Another time the Saint sent his monks to bring faggots from the field of a certain peasant for the construction of a hospice. And when they came back to the Saint with their transport filled with the aforesaid cargo of twigs, and said that the peasant was very much displeased indeed on account of the loss of them, the Saint at once gives directions and says, "Then lest we should put a stumbling-block in that man's way, let there be taken to him from us twice three pecks of barley, and let him sow it at once in his ploughed land."

And when, according to the bidding of the Saint, it was sent to the peasant, Findchan by name, and set before him with such a commendation, he thankfully accepts it, but says, "How can a field do any good if sown after midsummer, contrary to the nature of this land?"

His wife, on the other hand, says, "Do according to the command of the Saint, to whom the Lord will grant whatsoever he may ask of Him."

But they that were sent added this also at the same time, saying, "St. Columba, who hath sent us to thee with this present, entrusted also this instruction through us about thy field, saying, 'Let that man trust in the omnipotence of God: his field, although sown after twelve days of the month of June have passed, will be reaped in the beginning of the month of August.' "

The peasant obeys, both ploughing and sowing, and the harvest which he sowed against hope at the aforesaid time he got in ripe in the beginning of the month of August, to the great admiration of all the neighbours, according to the word of the Saint.

The Rule of Columba

Be alone in a separate place near a chief city, if thy conscience is not prepared to be in common with the crowd.

Be always naked in imitation of Christ and the Evangelists.

Whatsoever little or much thou possessest of anything, whether food or drink or clothing, let it be at the command of the senior and at his disposal, for it is not befitting a religious to have any distinction of property with his own free brother.

Let a fast place with one door enclose thee.

A few religious men to converse with thee of God and his Testament, to visit thee on days of solemnity: to strengthen thee in the Testaments of God and the narratives of the Scriptures.

A person who would talk with thee in idle words, or of the world, or who murmurs at what he cannot remedy or prevent, but who would distress thee more, should he be a tattler between friends and foes, thou shalt not admit him to thee, but at once give him thy benediction, should he deserve it.

Let thy servant be a discreet religious, not tale-bearing man, who is ready to attend continually on thee, with moderate labour of course, but always ready.

Yield submission to every rule that is of devotion.

A mind prepared for red martyrdom.

A mind fortified and steadfast for white martyrdom.

Forgiveness from the heart for everyone.

Constant prayers for those who trouble thee.

Fervor in singing the office for the dead, as if every faithful dead was a particular friend of thine.

Hymns for souls to be sung standing.

Let thy vigils be constant from eve to eve, under another's direction.

Three labours in the day — prayers, work and reading.

Thy work to be divided into three parts, thine own work and the work of thy place as regards its real wants: secondly thy share of the brethren's work: lastly, to help the neighbours by instruction or writing or sewing garments or whatever labour they may be in want of, *ut Dominus ait,* "*Non apparebis ante me vacuus.*"

Everything in its proper order: *Nemo enim coronabitur nisi qui legitime certaverit.*

Follow almsgiving before all things.

Take not of food until thou art hungry.

Sleep not till thou feelest desire.

Speak not except on business.

Every increase which comes to thee in lawful meals, or in wearing apparel, give it for pity to the brethren that want it, or to the poor in like manner.

The love of God with all thy heart and with all thy strength.

The love of thy neighbour as thyself.

Abide in the Testaments of God throughout all times.
Thy measure of prayer shall be until thy tears come;
Or thy measure of work of labour till thy tears come:
Or thy measure of thy work of labour, or of thy genuflections until thy perspiration come often, if thy tears are not free.

Translated by Dr Reeves

Delightful would it be to me to be in Uchd Ailiun★
   On the pinnacle of a rock,
That I might often see
   The face of the ocean;
That I might see its heaving waves
   Over the wide ocean,
When they chant music to their Father
   Upon the world's course;
That I might see its level of sparkling strand,
   It would be no cause of sorrow;
That I might hear the roar by the side of the church
   Of the surrounding sea;
That I might see its noble flocks
   Over the watery ocean;
That I might see the sea-monsters,
   The greatest of all wonders;
That I might see its ebb and flood
   In their career;
That my musical name might be, I say,
   Cul ri Erin;†

★ An Irish headland.   †"He who turned his back on Ireland."

That contrition might come upon my heart
  Upon looking at her;
That I might bewail my evils all,
  Though it were difficult to compute them;
That I might bless the Lord
  Who conserves all,
Heaven with its countless bright orders,
  Land, strand and flood;
That I might search the books all,
  That would be good for my soul;
At times kneeling to beloved Heaven;
  At times psalm singing;
At times contemplating the King of Heaven,
  Holy the Chief;
At times at work without compulsion,
  That would be delightful.
At times plucking duilisc from the rocks;
  At times fishing;
At times giving food to the poor;
  At times in a solitary cell.

Attributed to Columba
Translated by Eugene O'Curry

The Seafaring Monks

Wondrous the warriors who abode in Hi,
Thrice fifty in monastic rule,
With their boats along the main-sea,
Three score men a-rowing.

From the Book of Lismore

Columba Calms the Storm at Sea

At another time, the holy man began to be in peril by
the sea, for the entire hull of the ship was heavily struck,
and violently dashed about on the huge mountains of
the waves, while a great tempest of winds bore upon
them on every side. Then by chance the sailors say to
the Saint as he is endeavouring with them to empty the
bilge-hole, "What thou now doest doth not greatly
profit us in our danger; thou shouldest rather pray for
us now that we are perishing." On hearing which, he
ceases to empty out the bitter water, the green sea-
wave, but begins to pour out sweet and earnest prayer
to the Lord. Wondrous to say, in the same moment of
time which the Saint, standing at the prow with his
hands stretched out to heaven, besought the Almighty,
the whole storm of wind and the raging of the sea,
being stilled more quickly than can be said, eased, and
at once there followed a most tranquil calm. But they
who were in the ship were amazed, and rendering
thanks with great wonder, glorified the Lord in the
Holy and famous man.

The Consolation of the Monks

Among these memorable utterances of the prophetic
spirit, it seems not out of place also to make a record
in our little narrative of a certain spiritual consolation
which the monks of St Columba perceived on one
occasion, when his spirit met them by the way. For
once the brethren, returning to the monastery in the
evening after their harvest work, and arriving in that
place named Cuuleilne, which place is said to be
midway between the western plain of the island of Iona
and our monastery, appeared each to feel within himself
something wonderful and unusual, which, however,
not one of them dared in any way to intimate to
another. And so for some days they perceived it in the
same place, and at the same evening hour. But in those
days St Baithene was the superintendent of labours
among them, and he thus spoke to them one day,
saying, "Now, brethren, if ye perceive any unusual and
unexpected marvel in this place, midway between the
harvest-field and the monastery, ye ought each of you
to declare it."

Then one of them, a senior, says, "According to thy
bidding I will tell what has been shown to me in this
place; for in these days that are passing, and even now,
I perceive some fragrance of wondrous odour, as if that
of all flowers collected into one; also some burning as
of fire, not penal, but somehow sweet; moreover also
a certain unaccustomed and incomparable gladness
diffused in my heart, which suddenly consoles me in a
wonderful manner and gladdens me to such a degree
that I can remember no more the sadness, nor any

labour. Yea, even the load, although a heavy one, which I am carrying on my back from this place until we come to the monastery, is so lightened, I know not how, that I do not perceive that I have a load at all."

What more shall I say? So all the harvest-workers declare, one by one, each for himself, that they have had sensations in all respects as one of them had narrated openly, and all together on bended knees besought of St. Baithene that he would inform them, in their ignorance, of the cause and origin of the wondrous consolation which he and the rest were alike perceiving. To whom therefore he gave this reply, saying, "Ye know that our father Columba thinks anxiously about us, and takes it sadly that we come to him so late; but he being mindful of our labour, and by reason that he comes not to us in the body, his spirit meets our steps, and it is that which gladdens us with such consolations."

On hearing these words, the brethren, still kneeling, with joy unspeakable and with hands spread out to heaven, venerate Christ in the holy man.

The Visitation of the Holy Spirit

Another time, while the holy man was sojourning in
Hinba island, the grace of holy inspiration was poured
out upon him in an abundant and incomparable
manner, and wonderfully continued with him for three
days; so that, for three days and as many nights, he
remained within a house which was locked up and filled
with celestial light, would suffer no man to come near
him, and neither did eat nor drink. And from this
house, mark you, rays of intense brightness were seen
at night breaking out through the chinks of the doors
and the keyholes. Some spiritual songs also, which had
not been heard before, were then heard as they were
being sung by him. But he himself also, as he afterwards
declared before a very few persons, saw, openly manifested, many secret things, hidden ever since the foundation of the world. Some obscure and most difficult
passages of the sacred Scriptures appeared plain; and in
that light were more clearly manifested to the eyes of
his most pure heart. He lamented that Baithene his
foster-son was not present; had he chanced to be there
in those three days, he might have written down many
things from the lips of the blessed man; mysteries
unknown by other men, either concerning past ages,
or those which were next to follow; and also some
explanation of the sacred volumes. Baithene, however,
could not be present, being detained by contrary winds
in the Egean island [Eigg] until those three days and as
many nights of that incomparable and glorious visi-
tation came to a close.

The Altus of Columba

Columba is said to have written many poems and hymns, both in Irish and in Latin, but they seem to have come down through several centuries by oral tradition, so the authenticity of the existing written forms is not assured. Only three of his Latin hymns remain, preserved in the Liber Hymnorum, which probably dates to the eleventh century. The most famous of these is the "Altus," taking its name from the first word; each of the twenty-two stanzas begins in order with a letter of the alphabet, perhaps as an aid to the memory. Two stanzas are given here: the A (Altus), translated by the Rev. Anthony Mitchell; and the R (Regis), translated by Helen Waddell.

Ancient of Days; enthroned on high!
   The Father unbegotten He,
Whom space containeth not, nor time;
   Who was, and is, and aye shall be:
And one-born Son, and Holy Ghost,
   Who co-eternal glory share;
One only God of Persons Three,
   We praise, acknowledge, and declare.

Day of the king most rightous,
   The day is nigh at hand,
The day of wrath and vengeance,
   And darkness on the land.
Day of thick clouds and voices,
   Of mighty thundering,
A day of narrow anguish
   And bitter sorrowing.
The love of women's over,
   And ended is desire,
Men's strife with men is quiet,
   And the world lusts no more.

Two Ancient Prophecies

Seven years before the Judgment
The sea shall sweep over Erin at one tide,
And over blue-green Isla.
But the Island of Columba
Shall swim above the flood.

In Iona of my heart, Iona of my love,
Instead of monks' voices shall be lowing of cattle;
But ere the world comes to an end,
Iona shall be as it was.

Columbanus: Naught But a Road

O life, how greatly thou hast cheated, how many thou
hast blinded, how many led astray. Thou fliest, and art
nothing: seen, thou art a shadow: in stay, a wreath of
smoke that daily vanished and daily comes again: in
coming, thou fliest, in flying, comest: unlike in thy
event, alike in thy beginning: unlike in thy bestowing,
alike in thy passing: to fools a sweetness, bitter to the
wise. Yet thou hadst been true, if the sin of the first
transgression had not broken thee, left thee tottering
and mortal. A road to life art thou, not Life. . . . And
there is no man makes his dwelling in the road, but
walks there: and those who fare along the road have

their dwelling in the fatherland. So thou art naught, O mortal life, naught but a road, a fleeting ghost, an emptiness, a cloud uncertain and frail, a shadow and a dream.

From a sermon of Columbanus,
Translated by Helen Waddell

Some Sayings of Columbanus

Let us be careful that no image but that of God take shape in our souls.

The wise man meditates on the end of his life.

The man to whom little is not enough will not benefit from more.

Be hard among pleasant things, be gentle among harsh things.

Let the tongue have its reins firmly in the heart.

He who tramples the world tramples on himself.

From various writings of Columbanus

Columbanus' Rowing Song

Lo, cut in forests, the driven keel passes on the
      stream
Of twin-horned Rhine, and glides as if anointed on
      the flood.
Ho, my men! Let ringing echo sound our Ho!
The winds raise their blasts, the dread rain works
      its woe,
But men's ready strength conquers and routs the
      storm.
Ho, my men! Let ringing echo sound our Ho!
For the clouds yield to endurance, and the storm
      yields,
Effort tames them all, unwearied toil conquers all
      things.
Ho, my men! Let ringing echo sound our Ho!
Bear, and preserve yourselves for favouring
      fortune,
Ye that have suffered worse, to these also God shall
      give an end.
Ho, my men! Let ringing echo sound our Ho!
Thus the hated foe deals as he wearies our hearts,
And by ill temptation shakes the inward hearts
      with rage.
Let your mind, my men, recalling Christ, sound
      Ho!

Written by Columbanus on his trip up the Rhine,
Translated by G. S. M. Walker

Saint Gall Finds a Spot for his Cell

St Gall was one of the twelve missionary peregrini who came from
Bangor with St Columbanus and helped in the establishment of the
renowned monastery of Luxeuil in Burgundy. After many years
there, the Irish clerics were expelled in 610 by their former patron,
the King of Burgundy, and resumed their missionary wanderings,
eventually going up the Rhine to Lake Constance. There Gall
became ill and remained, while Columbanus went on to Italy and
his final foundation at Bobbio. Gall recovered, and became possessed
with a burning desire to spend the rest of his days in a solitary
retreat in the wilderness south of the lake.

The athlete of God, taking with him the things his
guide had told him, set out on his way after offering
prayer, the deacon before him. They pursued their
journey throughout the day, and as the sun was near
its setting they came to the stream called Steinaha and
followed its course till they reached the cliff from which
it descends with violence, forming a pool below. Here
they saw a quantity of fish and they threw their nets
into the water and caught some. Then they kindled a
fire and the deacon boiled the fish and laid out the bread
on top of the wallet. St. Gall meantime retired a short
distance to pray, and as he was walking through the
tangled thorn-brake, his foot caught and he fell to earth.
The deacon ran to lift him up; but the man of God,
filled with the spirit of prophecy, said: "Suffer me to
be; this shall be my rest for ever; here will I dwell, for
I have chosen it" (Ps. 132:15).

And after praying, he rose to his feet, and taking a
hazel-twig he formed it into a cross and fixed it in the
ground. He had hanging round his neck a satchel which

contained relics of the blessed Mary the Mother of God and the holy martyrs Maurice and Desiderius. He suspended this satchel from the cross and called the deacon; both prostrated themselves in prayer. When he had ended his prayer, as the sun was now setting and the day near its close, they partook at last of food, giving thanks to God before and after meal, and then strewed couches for themselves on the ground to rest awhile. But as soon as the Saint deemed his companion sound asleep, he arose and prostrating himself (with arms outstretched) in the form of a cross before the satchel, poured forth fervent prayers to the Lord. While he was thus engaged, a bear came down from the mountains and began stealthily to pick up the crumbs and broken morsels which they had let fall during their repast. When the man of God saw this, he said to the beast: "In the name of the Lord, I command thee to take up a log and throw it on the fire."

The monster turned at his bidding and brought a stout log and threw it into the fire. Thereupon the kindhearted saint went to his wallet and, drawing forth a loaf yet untouched from his scanty store, gave it to his servitor, saying: "In the name of my Lord Jesus Christ, depart from this valley; thou art free to range the hills and mountains around at will so long as thou doest no harm to man or beast in this spot."

The deacon meantime, feigning sleep, had watched how the beloved of God dealt with the beast; at last he rose and threw himself at the Saint's feet, saying: "Now I know of a truth that the Lord is with thee, since even the beasts of the wilderness obey thee."

But the Saint answered him: "Take heed that thou tell no man of this till thou see the glory of God."

From Walahfrid Strabo

The Vision of Fursey

Whilst Sigebert still governed the kingdom [East Anglia], there came out of Ireland a holy man called Fursey renowned both for his words and actions, and remarkable for singular virtues, being desirous to live a stranger for our Lord, wherever an opportunity should offer. . . . This man was of noble Irish blood, but much more noble in mind than in birth. From his boyish years, he had particularly applied himself to reading sacred books and following monastic discipline, and, as is most becoming to holy men, he carefully practised all that he learned was to be done.

In course of time, he build himself a monastery wherein he might with more freedom indulge his heavenly studies. There, falling sick, as the book about his life informs us, he fell into a trance, and, quitting his body from the evening till the cock crew, he was found worthy to behold the choirs of angels and hear the praises which are sung in heaven. . .

But there is one thing among the rest which we have thought may be beneficial to many if inserted in this history. When he had been lifted up on high, he was ordered by the angels that conducted him to look back upon the world. Upon which, casting his eyes downward, he saw, as it were, a dark and obscure valley underneath him. He also saw four fires in the air, not far distant from each other. Asking the angels what fires these were, he was told that they were the fires which would kindle and consume the world. One of them was falsehood, when we do not fulfil that which we promised in baptism, to renounce the Devil and all his works. The next of covetousness, when we prefer the riches of the world to the love of heavenly things. The third of discord, when we make no effort not to offend the minds of our neighbours, even in needless things. The fourth of iniquity, when we look upon it as no crime to rob and defraud the weak.

These fires, increasing by degrees, extended so as to meet one another, and being joined, became an immense flame. When it drew near, fearing for himself, Fursey said to the angel, "Lord, behold the fire draws near me."

The angel answered, "That which you did not kindle shall not burn you; for though this appears to be a terrible and great fire, yet it tries every man according to the merit of his works; for every man's concupiscence shall burn in the fire; for as every one burns in the body through unlawful pleasure, so when discharged of the body, he shall burn in the punishment which he has deserved."

Then he saw one of the three angels, who had been his conductors throughout both visions, go before and divide the flame of fire, while the other two, flying about on both sides, defended him from the danger of that fire. He also saw devils flying through the fire, raising conflagrations of wars against the just. Then followed accusations of the wicked spirits against him, the defence of the good angels in his favour, and a more extended view of the heavenly troops; as also of holy men of his own nation, who, as he had long since been informed, had been deservedly advanced to the degree of priesthood, from whom he heard many things that might be salutary to himself, or to all others that would listen to them. When they had ended their discourse and returned to heaven with the angelic spirits, the three angels remained with the blessed Fursey, of whom we have spoken before, and who were to bring him back to his body. And when they approached the aforesaid immense fire, the angel divided the flames, as he had done before; but when the man of God came to the passage so opened amidst the flames, the unclean spirits, laying hold of one of those whom they tormented in the fire, threw him at Fursey, and, touching his shoulder and jaw, burned them. He knew the man, and called to mind that he had received his garment when he died; and the angel, immediately laying hold, threw the man back into the fire, and the malignant enemy said, "Do not reject him whom you before received; for as you accepted the goods of him who was a sinner, so you must partake of his punishment."

The angel replying said, "He did not receive the same through avarice, but in order to save the man's soul."

The fire ceased, and the angel, turning to him, added, "That which you kindled burned in you; for had you not received the goods of this person that died in his sins, his punishment would not burn in you." And proceeding in his discourse, he gave him wholesome advice for what ought to be done towards the salvation of such as repented on their death-bed.

Being afterwards restored to his body, throughout the whole course of his life he bore the mark of the fire which he had felt in his soul, visible to all men on his shoulder and jaw; and the flesh publicly showed, in a wonderful manner, what the soul had suffered in private. He always took care, as he had done before, to persuade all men to the practice of virtue, as well by his example as by preaching. But as for the matter of his visions, he would only relate them to those who, from holy zeal and desire of reformation, wished to learn the same. An ancient brother of our monastery is still living, who is wont to declare that a very sincere and religious man told him that he had seen Fursey himself in the province of the East Angles, and heard those visions from his mouth; adding that though it was in most sharp winter weather, and a hard frost, and the man was sitting in a thin garment when he related it, yet he sweated as if it had been in the greatest heat of summer, either through excessive fear, or spiritual consolation.

From the Venerable Bede

Aidan comes to Lindisfarne

On the arrival of Aidan, King Oswald appointed him his episcopal see in the Isle of Lindisfarne, as he desired. Which place, as the tide ebbs and flows, twice a day is enclosed by the waves of the sea like an island; and again, twice in the day, when the shore is left dry, becomes connected to the land. The king also humbly and willingly in all cases giving ear to his admonitions, industriously applied himself to build and extend the Church of Christ in his kingdom. And while the bishop, who was not skilful in the English tongue, preached the Gospel, it was most delightful to see the king himself interpreting the word of God to his commanders and ministers, for he had perfectly learned the language of the Scots during his long banishment.

From the Venerable Bede

Of the Life of Bishop Aidan

From the aforesaid island [Iona], and college of monks, was Aidan sent to instruct the English nation in Christ, having received the dignity of a bishop at the time when Segenius, abbot and priest, presided over that monastery. Among other instructions for the holy life, he left the clergy a most salutary example of abstinence and continence, and it was the highest commendation of his doctrine, with all men, that he taught no otherwise than he and his followers had lived. He neither sought nor loved any thing of this world, but delighted in distributing immediately among the poor whatsoever was given him by the kings or rich men of the world. He was wont to traverse both town and country on foot, never on horseback, unless compelled by some urgent necessity; and wherever in his way he saw any, either rich or poor, he invited them, if heathen, to embrace the mystery of the faith; or if they were believers, he strengthened them in the faith and stirred them by words and actions to alms and good works.

His course of life was so different from the slothfulness of our times, that all those who bore him company, whether they were shorn monks or laymen, were employed in meditation, that is, either in reading the Scriptures, or learning psalms. This was the daily employment of himself and all that were with him, wheresoever they went; and if it happened, which was but seldom, that he was invited to eat with the king, he went with one or two clerks, and having taken a small repast, made haste to be gone with them, either to read or write.

From the Venerable Bede

Aidan's Gift Horse

King Oswin had given an extraordinarily fine horse to Bishop Aidan, which he might either use in crossing rivers or in performing a journey upon any urgent necessity, though he was wont to travel ordinarily on foot. Some short time after, a poor man meeting him and asking alms, he immediately dismounted and ordered the horse, with all his royal furniture, to be given to the beggar; for he was very compassionate, a great friend to the poor, and, as it were, the father of the wretched. This being told to the king, when they were going in to dinner, he said to the bishop, "Why would you, my lord Bishop, give the poor man that royal horse, which was necessary for your use? Had not we many other horses of less value, and of other sorts, which would have been good enough to give to the poor, without giving that horse which I had particularly chosen for yourself?" To whom the bishop instantly answered, "What is it you say, O king? Is that foal of a mare more dear to you than the child of God?" Upon this they went in to dinner, and the bishop sat in his place; but the king, who was come from hunting, stood warming himself, with his attendants, at the fire. Then, whilst he was warming himself and thinking on what the bishop had said to him, suddenly he ungirt his sword and gave it to a servant, and, in a hasty manner, he fell down at the bishop's feet, beseeching him to forgive him: "For from this time forward," said he, "I will never speak any more of this, nor will I judge of what or how much of our money you shall give to the sons of God." The bishop was much moved at this sight, and starting up, raised him, saying that he was entirely reconciled to him, if he would sit down to his meat and lay aside all sorrow. The king, at the bishop's request, began to be merry, but the bishop, on the other hand, grew so melancholy as to shed tears. His priest then asked him in the language of his country, which the king and his servants did not understand, why he wept. "I know," said he, "that the king will not live long; for I never before saw so humble a king, whence I feel that he will soon be snatched out of this life, because this nation is not worthy of such a ruler." Not long after, the bishop's prediction was fulfilled by the king's death, as has been said above. But Bishop Aidan was also taken out of this world, twelve days after the king he loved, on the 31st of August [651], to receive the eternal reward of his labours from our lord.

From the Venerable Bede

Cuthbert's Island Hermitage

Now after Cuthbert had completed many years in that same monastery [Lindisfarne], he joyfully entered into the remote solitudes which he had long desired, sought, and prayed for, with the good will of the abbot and also of the brethren. For he rejoiced because, after a long and blameless active life, he was now held worthy to rise to the repose of divine contemplation. . . . Now indeed at the first beginnings of his solitary life, he retired to a certain place in the outer precincts of the monastery which seemed to be more secluded. But when he had fought there in solitude for some time with the invisible enemy, by prayer and fasting, he sought a place of combat further and more remote from mankind, aiming at greater things. There is an island called Farne in the middle of the sea, some miles away to the south-east of the half-island of Lindisfarne, shut in on the landward side by very deep water and on the seaward side by the boundless ocean. No one had been able to dwell alone undisturbed upon this island before Cuthbert the servant of the Lord, on account of the phantoms of demons who dwelt there; but when the soldier of Christ entered, armed with the "helmet of salvation, the shield of faith, and the sword of the spirit which is the word of God, all the fiery darts of the wicked one" were quenched, and the wicked foe himself was driven far away together with the whole crowd of his satellites. This soldier of Christ, as soon as he had become monarch of the land he had entered and had overcome the army of the usurpers, built a city fitted for his rule, and in it houses equally suited to the city. It is a structure almost round in plan, measuring about four or five poles from wall to wall; the wall itself on the outside is higher than a man standing upright; but inside he made it much higher by cutting away the living rock, so that the pious inhabitant could see nothing except the sky from his dwelling, thus restraining the lust of both the eyes and the thoughts and lifting the whole bent of his mind to higher things. He made this same wall, not of cut stone nor of bricks and mortar, but of unworked stone and turf which he had removed from the excavation in the middle of his dwelling. Some of these stones were so great that it would seem to have been scarcely possible for four men to have lifted them, but nevertheless he was found to have brought them thither from elsewhere with angelic aid, and to have placed them in the wall. He had two buildings in his dwelling place, namely an oratory and

133

another habitation suitable for common uses. He finished the walls by cutting and digging away the natural soil both inside and outside, and he placed on them roofs of rough-hewn timber and straw. . . .

Now when this same dwelling place and these chambers had been built with the help of his brethren, Cuthbert the man of God began to dwell alone. At first, indeed, he used to go forth from his cell to meet the brethren who came to him, and to minister to them. And when he had devoutly washed their feet in warm water, he was sometimes compelled by them to take off his shoes and to allow them to wash his feet. For he had so far withdrawn his mind from the care of his body and fixed it on the care of his soul alone that, having once been shod with the boots of skin that he was accustomed to use, he would wear them for whole months together. And let it be said that once he had put his boots on at Easter, he did not take them off until Easter came round again a year later, and then only for the washing of the feet which takes place on Maundy Thursday. So, on account of the frequent genuflections he made at prayer while wearing his boots, he was found to have a long and thickish callus at the junction of his feet and his shins. Then, when his zeal for perfection grew, he shut himself up in the hermitage, and, remote from the gaze of men, he learned to live a solitary life of fasting, prayers and vigils, rarely having conversation from within his cell with visitors and that only through the window. At first he opened this and rejoiced to see and be seen by the brethren with whom he spoke; but as time went on, he shut even that, and opened it only for the sake of giving his blessing or for some other definite necessity.

From Bede's Life of St Cuthbert

Alcuin his Epitaph

Here halt, I pray you, make a little stay,
O wayfarer, to read what I have writ,
And know by my fate what thy fate shall be.
What thou art now, wayfarer, world-renowned,
I was: what I am now, so shalt thou be.
The world's delight I followed with a heart
Unsatisfied: ashes am I, and dust.

Wherefore bethink thee rather of thy soul
Than of thy flesh;—this dieth, that abides.
Dost thou make wide thy fields? in this small house
Peace holds me now: no greater house for thee.
Wouldst have thy body clothed in royal red?
The worm is hungry for that body's meat.
Even as the flowers die in a cruel wind,
Even so, O flesh, shall perish all thy pride.

Now in thy turn, wayfarer, for this song
That I have made for thee, I pray you, say:
"Lord Christ, have mercy on Thy servant here,"
And may no hand disturb this sepulchre,
Until the trumpet rings from heaven's height,
"O thou that liest in the dust, arise,
The Judge of the unnumbered hosts is here!"

Alcuin was my name: learning I loved.
O thou that readest this, pray for my soul.

Translated by Helen Waddell

Sedulius Scottus: Easter Sunday

Last night did Christ the Sun rise from the dark,
    The mystic harvest of the fields of God,
And now the little wandering tribes of bees
    Are brawling in the scarlet flowers abroad.
The winds are soft with birdsong; all night long
    Darkling the nightingale her descant told,
And now inside church doors the happy folk
    The Alleluia chant a hundredfold.
O father of thy folk, be thine by right
The Easter joy, the threshold of the light.

Translated by Helen Waddell

And the Life was the Light of Men

And the Life was the Light of men. The Son of God, O
blessed theologian, Whom earlier you called the Word,
now you name Life and Light. Not without reason are
the names changed, but in order to make known to us
different meanings. If indeed you have named the Son
of God the Word, it is because through Him the Father
spoke all things: "For He spake and it was done." Life
and Light, you named Him thereafter because the same
Son is truly the Life and Light of all things which were
made through Him. And what does He light? Not other

136

than Himself and His Father. He is the Light, therefore, and illuminates Himself. He reveals Himself to the world, He manifests Himself to the ignorant.

The light of divine knowledge receded from the world when man abandoned God. Since then the eternal Light reveals itself to the world in a twofold way: through Scripture and through creature. For in no other way may divine knowledge be renewed in us, but through the letters of divine Scripture and the species of creature. Learn, therefore, to understand these divine modes of expression and to conceive their meaning in your soul: therein you will know the Word. Observe with your bodily senses the forms and beauties of sensible things, and comprehend in them the Word of God. In all these things the truth will reveal to you naught but Him Who made all things, outside of Whom you have nothing to contemplate, for He Himself is All. For in all things which are, whatever is, is He. For, just as no substantial good exists outside Him, no essence or substance exists besides Him.

And the Life was the Light of men. Why does he add "the Light of men," as if the Light which is the light of the angels, the light of the created universe, the light of all visible and invisible existence, should be especially and peculiarly the Light of men? Is not, perhaps, the Word, animating all things, said to be especially and peculiarly the Light of men, because in man He declared Himself not only to humans, but also to the angels and to all creatures able to participate in divine Knowledge? For He did not come as an angel to the angels, nor as an angel to men, but as a man to both men and angels. And He came not in appearance alone, but in true humanity, which He took upon Himself completely, in unity of substance, and so presented Himself, His Knowledge, to all modes of knowing. Thus the Light of men is our Lord Jesus Christ, Who in His human nature manifested Himself to all rational and intellectual creatures, and revealed the hidden mysteries of His divinity, by which He is equal to the Father.

John Scotus Erigena,
From the Homily on the Prologue to the Gospel of St. John,
Translated by Christopher Bamford

The Holy Isles

*For William Irwin Thompson and all the friends he has united in
the abiding vision that is Lindisfarne.*

Lindisfarne

Those whose faces are turned always to the sun's rising
See the living light on its path approaching
As over the glittering sea where in tide's rising and
    falling
The sea-beasts bask, on the Isles of Farne
Aidan and Cuthbert saw God's feet walking
Each day towards all who on world's shores await his
    coming.
That we too, hand in hand, have received the unending
    morning.

Iona

Where, west of the sun, our loved remembered
    home?
Columba's Eire from Iona's strand
Land-under-wave beyond last dwindling speck
That drops from sight the parting ship
As mourners watch wave after wave break.
Sight follows on its golden wake
A dream returning to its timeless source, the heart
Where all remains that we have loved and known.

Kathleen Raine

Bibliography

Adamnan, *Prophecies, Miracles and Visions of St Columba*, Clarendon, Oxford 1895.

——, *Vita S. Columbae*, (*The Life of St Columba*) Edited from Dr Reeves' text by T. J. Fowler, Clarendon, Oxford 1894.

Bede, *Life of St Cuthbert*. From *Two Lives of St Cuthbert*, Trans. Bertram Colgrave, reprinted Greenwood, New York 1965.

——, *The Ecclesiastical History of the English Nation*, Everyman, London 1910.

Bergin, O. J. *Stories from Keating's History of Ireland*, Dublin 1910.

Bieler, Ludwig, "The Island of Scholars" *Revue du Moyen Age Latin*, 8:3, 1952.

Carmichael, Alexander (Ed.) *Carmina Gadelica*. 5 vols. Oliver & Boyd, Edinburgh 1900–54.

Carney, James (Trans.) *Medieval Irish Lyrics*, University of California Press, Berkeley 1967.

Carson, Molloy (Trans.) *Ancient Irish Lyrics*, VIIIth – XIIth Century, Emerald, Belfast 1955.

Chadwick Nora, *The Age of the Saints in the Celtic Church*, Oxford University Press, 1961.

Curtayne, Alice, *St Brigit of Ireland*, Sheed & Ward, New York 1954.

Dillon, Miles (Ed.) *Early Irish Society*, Mercier, Cork 1954.

Erigena, John Scotus, *Homily on the Prologue to the Gospel of Saint John*, Lindisfarne, West Stockbridge, Mass.

Flower, Robin, *The Irish Tradition*, Clarendon, Oxford 1947.

Hamlin, Ann, *see* Hughes, Kathleen & Ann Hamlin.

Hardinge, Leslie, *The Celtic Church in Britain*, S.P.C.K. London 1972.

Harney, Martin, *The Legacy of Saint Patrick*, St Paul, Boston, Mass, 1972.

Hughes, Kathleen, and Ann Hamlin, *Celtic Monasticism: The Modern Traveller to the Early Irish Church*, Seabury, New York 1981.

Lindisfarne Gospels.

Macleod, Fiona, *The Divine Adventure: Iona.* Duffield, New York 1910.

McNeill, John, *The Celtic Churches.* University of Chicago Press 1974.

Marsh, A. *St Patrick and his Writings*, Dundalk 1966.

Massingham, H. J. *The Tree of Life*, Chapman & Hall, London 1943.

Menzies, Lucie, *Saint Columba of Iona*, Dent, London & Toronto 1920.

Meyer, Kuno (Trans.) *Selections from Ancient Irish Poetry*, Constable, London 1911.

O'Meara, John, J. *The Voyage of St Brendan*, Dolmen, Dublin 1978.

Patrick, *Confessions.* From *The Legacy of Saint Patrick*, Trans. Martin Harney, St. Paul, Boston 1972.

Plummer, Charles (Ed. & Trans.) *Lives of Irish Saints*, 2 vols. Oxford University Press 1922.

Ryan, John, *Irish Monasticism*, Cornell University Press, Ithica, New York, 1972.

Sherman, Katherine, *The Flowering of Ireland*, Little, Brown, Boston, Mass. 1981.

Stokes, Margaret, *Early Christian Art in Ireland*, Chapman, London n.d.

Stokes, Whitley (Ed. & Trans.) *Lives of the Saints from the "Book of Lismore"*, Clarendon, Oxford 1890.

——, *The Tripartite of St Patrick.* Eyre & Spottiswoode, London 1887.

Strabo, Walahfrid, *De Vita Sancti Galli* (The Life of St Gall) Trans. Maud Joynt, S.P.C.K. London 1927.

Stranks, C. J. *The Life and Death of St Cuthbert*, S.P.C.K. London 1964.

Taylor, John W. *The Coming of the Saints*, Methuen, London 1906.

Taylor, Thomas (Trans.) *The Life of St Samson of Dol*, S.P.C.K. London 1925.

Waddell, Helen (Trans.) *Mediaeval Latin Lyrics*, Holt, New York 1929.

——, *More Latin Lyrics*, Norton, New York 1977.

Walker, G. S. M. (Ed. & trans.) *Sancti Columbani Opera*, Dublin Institute of Advanced Studies, 1967.

Wilson, J. *Life of Columba*, Clonmore & Reynolds, Dublin 1954.

Wyatt, Isobel, "Goddess into Saint" *The Golden Blade*, 1963.

Yeats, W. B. *Collected Poems*, Macmillan, New York 1956.